For Judy —

Hope this proves

helpful !

SBWC '98

Judy Pochini
424 Las Alturas
Santa Barbara, Ca 93103

Double Your Creative Power!

Make Your Subconscious
A Partner in the Writing Process

BY S.L. STEBEL

Ruminations on the Art of Fiction
Including a User-Friendly
Supplement for Novel, Play and
Screenwriters plus a Short, Easy
Course in Film Writing, and of
Course, the Fundamentals.

ALLEN A. KNOLL, PUBLISHERS

First Edition
Second Impression, 1997

Library of Congress Cataloging-in-Publication Data

Stebel, S. L.
    Double your creative power : make your subconscious a partner in
the writing process : ruminations on the art of fiction, including a
user-friendly supplement for novel, play, and screen writers, plus a
short, easy course in film writing, and, of course, the fundamentals
/ by S.L. Stebel. -- 1st ed.
        p.   cm.
    ISBN 1-888310-20-0
    1. Authorship.   I. Title.
PN151.S82   1996
808'.02--dc20

96-17138
CIP

Text typeface is Bembo, 12 point
Printed on 60-pound Lakewood white, acid-free paper
Case bound with Kivar 9, Smyth Sewn

In homage to Aristotle, Robert Penn Warren, Somerset Maugham, Gerald Heard, Theodore Reik, James M. Cain and Ray Bradbury

…and dedicated to all those hard-working participants in writing workshops I have conducted around the world who have served as enthusiastic subjects in an ongoing, movable laboratory to test the theories set forth in this book.

Also By S.L. Stebel

Novels

The Collaborator
The Widowmaster (with Robert Weverka)
The Vorovich Affair
Spring Thaw
The Boss's Wife

Biography

The Shoe Leather Treatment

Films

Dreams of Marianne (Mirrors)
The Revolution of Antonio De Leon (with Robert Weverka)
Picnic at Hanging Rock (script consultant)
Storm Boy (script consultant)

Plays

The Way Out (with Charles Rome Smith)
Fathers Against Sons
Next in Line
Breeding

CONTENTS

INTRODUCTION I

I. WOOING THE MUSE. 7
    1. Once upon a time, etc. 7
    2. Getting the idea: How to find
    your secret story. 9

II. DEVELOPING THE IDEA. 16
    1. Staking out the territory. 16
    2. Before creating the narrative
    (story) line. 17
    3. Creating the story line. 19
    4. Making sense of (reviewing)
    the story line. 22
    5. Caring about the protagonist. 27
    6. Organizing the material: strengthening
    a story's bones. 29
    7. The story 'hook.' 32
    8. Structuring stories for
    maximum suspense. 34
    9. Mystery vs. suspense. 35

III. STORYTELLING TECHNIQUES & DEVICES. 38
    1. Where does the story begin? 38
    2. Prologues, their uses & functions. 40
    3. Points of view. 42
    4. Character motivation. 45
    5. Keep a continuing biography. 46
    6. The emotional arc. 47
    7. Exposition, when to use. 49
        a. exposition avoidance techniques. 51

8. The necessity of foreshadowing. 52
9. Rewriting. 53
   a. The 'step' outline. 56
   b. How many rewrites? 58
10. The final polish. 60

IV. THE ART OF STORYTELLING. 63
1. Opening lines. 63
2. Pace and style. 65
3. Past or present: what tense to use? 66
4. P.O.V. revisited. 68
5. Flashbacks, flashforwards, etc. 71
6. Common mistakes. 73
7. Emotion, and its lack. 75
8. Logic & common sense. 77
9. Breaking the rules. 82
10. Titles. 83

V. ADAPTING YOUR WORK FOR STAGE OR SCREEN. 85
1. Should you, would you, could you? 85

VI. A SHORT EASY COURSE IN SCREENWRITING. 94
1. Should you? (revisited.) 118

VII. ENTERING THE MARKETPLACE. 122
1. Protecting your work. 124

VIII. MISCELLANY. 127
a. What about writing groups? 127

IX. REPRISING A FEW FUNDAMENTALS. 131

INTRODUCTION

Read many good books lately? Seen any terrific movies, small screen or large? Watched any plays whose dramas engage both intellect and emotion?

Or do you find yourself more frequently laying books aside unfinished and leaving theatres disappointed? Do you wonder why so very few stories enthrall and so many actually fail in fiction's primary functions—to instruct and entertain?

In all good stories authors use certain key elements in powerful and emotional ways. In bad stories—which seem to be proliferating exponentially—key elements, principally having to do with emotional identification and clarity, are lacking.

Most writers who've become successful have done so by hard work over many years, in a hit or miss procedure, writing by God or by guess. They know little about the process they practice, and, finally successful, care less. Or they may be fearful of tampering with the Act of Creation, afraid that whatever's worked so well for them in the past might of a sudden disappear.

In my own case I'd become successful in a similar fashion, without much understanding of how this had been accomplished. Though after a number of false starts I'd managed to publish a number of novels, had two plays, a screenplay, and a television movie-of-the-week produced, worked with stars such as Henry Fonda and Fred Astaire, directors like Peter Weir and Herbert Ross, was represented

1

by Don Congdon, a top literary agent, and top Hollywood agents at Creative Management Associates (now ICM), and Creative Artists Agency, I still approached every project in a state of high anxiety, not at all confident that the ideas I was developing would result in anything worthwhile. Each project made me feel as if I were sailing off into a great unknown, certain that at any moment I risked tumbling off the edge of the earth into the abyss of failure.

Then, while working on a screenplay at MGM studios, I was invited by a production head, John Graves, to join him in Australia. John had accepted an appointment as executive producer at the newly-founded South Australian film corporation, whose mission was to seek out talent and material that would result in world-class films. He asked me to become the corporation's executive script consultant.

We had met in screening rooms viewing movies so ineptly made they had been shelved. While restructuring those films to make them sufficiently coherent for distribution to secondary markets, we had learned to appreciate each other's abilities.

What I didn't know then was that my new job 'down under' not only entailed "consulting" on screenplays scheduled for production, but in addition I would be asked to bootstrap budding authors into professionalism by evaluating scripts, lecturing nationwide for the National Literature Board, and conducting writing workshops.

In 1975 there were few ways to apprentice in the Australian film and TV industry, it being far cheaper to import ready-made British and American product. What I was being asked to do was provide writers an equivalent alternative. That meant not only giving them a basic understanding of what made a story successful, but insight into how such stories were conceived and developed.

First, of course, I had to understand the creative processes writers underwent. And that led me to some urgent thinking about what actually takes place at various stages during the process leading from idea to completed work.

After a twenty hour plus flight and a welcoming party in which I was giddied not only by hearing myself described as an industry 'savior', but learned to dread the Aussie propensity for 'topping up' any glass even a milliliter less full—I was confronted in my new office with scripts stacked wall to wall and floor to ceiling (every writer in Australia, it seemed, had inundated the ambitious new Film Corporation with material.) My first, and immediately sobering task, was coming up with a way to deal with the submissions not only fast, but intelligibly.

Whether it was the pressures of time and circumstance, the drastic, upside down shift in gravitational pull (I was, after all, on the other side of the earth), the pristine air (so pure, all colors seemed startlingly primary) or the visit to an aborigine encampment, where I struggled to understand an oral storyteller's concept of 'dream time'—whether it was, in fact, some or all of these things, I don't know, but the sought after insight suddenly struck me.

WRITE WHAT YOU FEEL

What we know best are our own emotions.

It's not write what you know, I realized. It's write what you feel.

Every individual's range of emotional responses is common to every other individual. Anyone observing babies and toddlers over any period of time can see every emotion being wordlessly played out, from happiness to rage, delight to frustration, and will witness, on those innocent faces, acts of destructive behavior as well as expressions of love.

WRITING PROCESS IS A SEARCH FOR MEANING

Knowing that we possess this wide emotional range is not enough, however. While endeavoring to come up with a method of gaining access to the emotions for story-telling purposes, it eventually became clear to me also that the writing process itself is a search for meaning. And that meaning can only be discovered in the subconscious.

When I first dreamed of becoming a writer, I despaired of creating work of any significance, thinking I hadn't had enough experience, or background, or learning. I believed I was about an inch deep, and had nothing, or at least nothing of importance, to say.

Now I know better. Nothing is about nothing. Everything is about something. Every individual, after day one, carries, deep within, emotional baggage packed full of past responses to situations and events. The trick is to decipher what the writer's muse (otherwise known as the subconscious) is saying.

In order to do this we must learn to read our own entrails—in other words, be able to decipher what our own words mean. For words can obscure as well as reveal. Give a writer a decoding tool with which to translate what his or her own subconscious is saying, and not only will stories of a unique and individual nature pour forth, but in releasing the emotions within, the sought after—longed for—sense of identification between writer and audience is achieved.

For some, the idea of trying to communicate with the subconscious is like sending a signal into outer space, hoping that in some remote galaxy someone or something will receive it, and, if we're lucky, send a signal back. In this case, of course, the regions we're going to explore are inside ourselves. And we no longer have to depend solely on luck, or, sadly, wait for 'inspiration.'

Not all, of course, are believers. The year after leaving Australia, during a workshop at the Santa Barbara Writers Conference, after I made the statement that it wasn't necessary to kill anyone in order to understand the urge to kill, since everyone has experienced a similar urge, a man stood up, identified himself as a minister of the faith, and disputed this. He himself had never felt such an urge, he said. I expressed disbelief. By the time the two of us had finished our little colloquy, the minister had to be restrained from rushing up to lay hands on me.

For too long fiction writing instructors have sent countless students away from their desks and out into the world seeking experience in hopes of finding subjects to write about.

Fortunately, the terrain to be explored is closer at hand, since writers who wish to be productive must live rather mundane existences (except of course where it counts, in the mind.) The most important search is an interior one.

The sooner the veils of mystery surrounding the creative process are blown away, the more likely the books, plays and screenplays we write will reach their fullest potential. And this, in turn, will greatly improve chances for commercial success.

For whatever reason—an urge to conform, to hook into what's popular—it's our conscious mind that keep the gates to our unique individuality, that is, our subconscious, doublebolted and locked tight. But to do the kind of creative work that will stand out in a crowd, we must open those gates and join with our subconscious in the search for meaning.

Not that this will always provide the writer with universal acceptance. An editor of a nationally respected literary publication, on a recent visit to my graduate seminar, stated that what most put him off in fictions submitted to him were "cautionary tales."

But all tales are cautionary. In art as in life, our journey's quest is to find the moral of the story. (Remember "an unexamined life is not worth living"?) Without a discovered theme, what's left is much ado about nothing, a tale told by an idiot, signifying nothing.

In the pages which follow, everything, from the method of interpreting your muse's emotional language, to the intelligent use of fictional techniques, will be devoted towards helping you create a coherent work whose art lies not in artifice, but in a profound rendering of human nature that has meaning for writer and reader alike.

What it is also intended to do is provide writers a means by which to avoid this prototypical rejection:

> Dear Contributor,
> Your work is both original and good.
> Unfortunately, that part which is good
> is not original, and that part which is
> original is not good.

I

WOOING THE MUSE

ONCE UPON A TIME, ETC.

In ways both mysterious and explicable, we are all connected.

From conception through birth, all fetuses progress through every mutation, including gill-breathing, which replicates our evolutionary migration from sea dwellers to land creatures.

Memories begin in the womb (some say even before.)

The myths of all cultures, while not interchangeable, are remarkably similar.

Stories of the creation of the universe vary mostly in degree, while tales of death and destruction, sacrifice and love, betrayal and redemption, are common to all cultures, populated by Gods whose larger than life personalities run the gamut from benevolent to mischievous, their behavior mimicked by populations the world over.

In the beginning was the Word. So says our Bible.

Gautama Buddha, five centuries before Christ, teaching the eightfold path as escape from mortality, placed the "right word" immediately after "right belief" and "right resolve."

But not everything was written.

The first storyteller may well have been a neanderthal separated from his own kind, stumbling out of the primeval mists towards a fire where neanderthals from another clan gathered to feast on the day's kill. Survival could have depended on answers to grunted queries such as "Who? How?" etc., which would lead, eons later, to Scheherazade's spellbinding of the Sultan, turning his head in order to retain her own.

Later, in keeping with this oral tradition, the oracles of Greece made prophecies and gave advice, usually in the form of riddles (which led to the creation of a priesthood to interpret those words, leading in turn to those practitioners we call critics.)

In the beginning was the Word. But almost from the beginning too, there have been images.

The 30,000 year old cave drawings discovered in France are a graphic display of one of mankind's earliest attempts to tell a story. This depiction of a successful hunt, once judged to be a form of historical record, has since been thought to be the practice of magic, in which the artists hoped that by depicting success they could create it.

Even today certain primitive tribes throw water into the air in the hopes of creating rain. And sports coaches teach a kind of Zen in which the athlete is encouraged to visualize winning moves before the performance.

All cultures have soothsayers and prophesizers, including Native American Indian shamans and African witch doctors. Other cultures have oral historians, passing on a tribe's traditions word of mouth (and who would deny those keepers of the faith a minor enhancement or melodramatic embellishment in order to keep their listeners' attention?)

The Australian aborigines conceive of a Dream Time, in which events from both past and future co-exist (a living demonstration of flashbacks and flashforwards.)

When we dream, which is a trip to our subconscious, it is almost always in pictures. When we want to interpret our dreams, however, those images have to be translated into words, the language of the writer.

Storytellers of every society, creators of fairy tales and parables, are direct descendants of those earlier makers of magic. *Once upon a time* are still magical words, promising an audience that if they will but momentarily suspend disbelief, a wondrous experience awaits them.

In the beginning was the Word. But later there was the Tower of Babel, a metaphor for our inability to understand one another, at least on a conscious level. Today, unfortunately, as writers we will remain confined to that tower, continuing to babble on, unless we learn how to communicate on a subconscious level.

It is the purpose of the following exercise to demonstrate how writers may do just that. By transporting ourselves into our own 'dream times', and learning how to interpret those dreams, writers can find the kind of ideas and concepts that will connect them to their readers in both mysterious (and therefore universal) but thoroughly explicable ways.

GETTING THE IDEA: HOW TO FIND YOUR SECRET STORY

Writer's block does not, repeat not, exist. Unless the writer has become catatonic, and cannot physically push words out of his mouth, there is no blockage.

If a writer can read, think and feel, there must still be words in the well. The brain has not gone dry. What is called block is more likely a fear that there is nothing left to say, nothing worthwhile to write about, which in turn causes the afflicted writer a loss of the will to write.

Lack of will comes mostly to those who have lost

touch with the drives which led them to writing in the first place. Many writers, feeling contempt for the demands of the marketplace, look down upon the work produced to fulfill those demands.

If a writer dislikes, or is depressed by the stories issuing from his/her writing place (usually caused because the stories have been contrived without any connection to the writer's most deeply felt beliefs), how can a reader be expected to like them?

WHERE DO IDEAS COME FROM?

Ever since the ancients wooed reluctant muses, writers have attempted a variety of rituals to call them forth. Some 'warm up' by writing nonsense or free verse, a kind of limbering up process intended to 'free' the mind.

Automatic writing and other stream-of-consciousness techniques are designed to put writers in touch with those mysterious 'sources' that provide inspiration. Imprisoned in our subconscious are thousands of ideas struggling to get out, hoping to be transformed into stories.

Truman Capote read the Bible to get his creative juices flowing. Every day Ernest Hemingway re-read his own work-in-progress from start to where he'd left off, as a kind of springboard from past into present that would stimulate his imagination. It was a way to take himself—his conscious self—by surprise. (If the writer is surprised, certainly the reader will be!) Ray Bradbury agrees, suggesting that we ought to "Write faster than we can think!"

Which started me thinking. 'Automatic writing' seemed to fall into a category similar to dream research. As guides to the subconscious both seemed murky and near incomprehensible, written in languages that defied translation.

But what if a method could be developed to expedite interpretation? What if a text produced automatically could be deciphered through a combination of logic and intuition?

I examined my own work patterns, trying to glean from accumulated notes reasons why this or that idea for a story had, or had not, progressed to a successful conclusion. Out of this re-thinking and synthesization of theories gleaned from the literature in the field, including the seminal work, *Listening with the Third Ear*, by Theodore Reik, an ongoing series of Sunday morning lectures by the British philosopher Gerald Heard dealing with interconnectedness, the experiences of other writers, and personal experimentation, what resulted was a method designed to overcome the internal censor that is the writer's most obstinate antagonist.

This method finally stems from a highly effective kind of solo **brainstorming** that attempts to engage the subconscious in a productive collaboration. This collaboration has not only helped me in my own work, but has also stimulated countless writers I have mentored who have gone on to publish novels and see their plays and screenplays produced.

SECRET STORY

My method is deceptively simple. It is best practiced alone. In workshop experiments at the Santa Barbara Writers Conference, some of the emotions released were so powerful participants were profoundly moved, and revelations of long suppressed memory, with attendant emotional upheavals, were not uncommon. (Also, with many participants seen leaving the workshop in tears, word quickly spread that I was a harsh critic.) Because I have no wish to function psycho-therapeutically, I have discontinued involving groups in what should be, for maximum results, a private undertaking.

PARTNERING WITH YOUR SUBCONSCIOUS, A 'HOW-TO' GUIDE

1. Immediately upon awakening in the morning, sit down at your regular writing place, and, without stopping to think, writing at white hot speed, put down everything that comes into your mind. Let the words pour out. Do not censor or edit or in any manner attempt to shape or form the material; put down every thought you can grab hold of any and every which way you can; do not attempt to write sentences that make sense. This is not writing in the normal sense; do otherwise and you may impede the flow.

Whatever you do, do not, repeat not, go back over the material, or reread what you have written, at any time in this initial writing process. Let one word trigger another. Let your mind "flash" on seeming irrelevancies. "Word associate" as freely and fast fast fast as you can. This procedure is the equivalent, Ray Bradbury has said, of "vomiting on the page." Try not to take him literally.

At some point you will get to an "end." Stop. Do not force the process. You should have anywhere from a page and a half (the absolute minimum) to five pages (there is no maximum as long as the flow remains uninterrupted.)

Do not read what you have written! This is vitally important. Under penalty of failure, do not look at the material. Put it away. Let it sit. Forget about it. Go on to your other work.

2. In about a week—no less, eventually more—pull out the material. Have a felt-tip pen or highlighter or soft lead pencil firmly in hand. As you read, circle those words and phrases that leap out of the page at you. List what

you've circled on a separate page.

Many you won't recall having written at all. These are "trigger" words, emotional telegrams, cries for help from stories struggling to get out. What is happening, of course, is that your subconscious is sending you messages. But those messages are in code. How do we interpret them?

3. Now, using **only** the circled words or phrases, discarding all others, repeat the process. Writing at flank speed, without stopping to think, flash on what you're reading. Put down every idea, feeling and thought associated with those trigger words. Again...hide the material away. And again, do not reread it.

4. A week or more later, repeat the process. A week or more after that, repeat the process again. Repeat the process as often as necessary. You will recognize the point at which you should stop this process: connections between the circled words are made; the outlines of a story will start to emerge.

If the method described is used honestly, stories **will** begin to take shape. Guaranteed. I'm not certain why. Perhaps because all of us, since childhood, have responded to linear narratives—those with beginnings, middles and ends, not necessarily in that order. (Worry about the order of the telling later.) Try "Child, stranger, lollipop, car." Unfortunately, we know how too many of those stories end.

Even if the story line remains unclear and unresolved, at the very least a metaphor will emerge—next to theme the most important clarification of your story.

Theme, or moral of the story, is the story's soul, and works best for the writer if stated simply, as in "Love Conquers All."

Metaphor identifies a story's subject: it's about violence, say, or greed, or love, or loss, etc., and is separate from the story's theme.

The narrative line is the spine to which the flesh of any narrative clings, even at its most episodic.

What is happening in this process is that your muse has freed a story that has long yearned for release from your subconscious. You're no longer dredging for ideas in an area that your spouse, or your lover, or your friends, or members of your writing group, think you should write. Nor are you acting in response to your dim understanding of the demands of the marketplace (by the time a trend is identifiable, that trend is probably finished anyway.)

What your subconscious is providing you is a story that only you can tell.

Because you now have an idea sprung from the deepest wellsprings of your being, it will have an emotional resonance that no amount of conscious work can bring.

Because of the idea's origins, it will be demonstrably original, and deeply felt.

We are each of us individual and unique as snowflakes; **ergo**, this uncensored idea will be individual and unique as well. (A few years ago, somewhere in the environs of Omaha, Nebraska, researchers thought they had found two snowflakes which were identical. Subsequent examination proved them wrong—and, I perhaps need not add, my use of this metaphor still correct.)

Benefits continue to accrue. Publishers and producers are on a continual hunt for original 'voices.' 'Voice', of course, in editorial parlance, is style. And since style **should** arise from the kind of story being told, you will, perforce, have a story and a style original enough to gain an editor's attention.

5. With the subject identified, and the idea spring-

ing clear, you can now bring all of your talent and skills to bear upon telling the story which your muse has presented you.

Whatever your current level of talent and ability, the proper use of the techniques offered in the following pages cannot help but raise your writing to another, higher level.

II

DEVELOPING THE STORY

STAKING OUT THE TERRITORY

At this point in the process, it is counterproductive to worry about writing well. Many people write well, and those who are serious about writing as a career usually have learned to write exceedingly well.

But for now, forget about style. Concentrate on story. Writers worry too much about style. Almost all of us, when we first began to dream of seeing our words in print, concentrated on writing 'pretty'. We brooded over images and figures of speech, working hard to describe scenes as they'd never been described before, 'worrying' words like a dog with a new bone.

There comes a time, however, when a writer has to assume that s/he's been practicing long enough—that is, sooner or later one has to believe one knows how to write. The question becomes academic. What we should be concentrating on is story. If the story is strong and individual, demanding to be told, the style will take care of itself. Style should be organic to each separate work (and not necessarily a 'signature' of a particular author). The kind of story being told, if it springs out of an author's deeply felt need to tell that story, produces its own unique 'style'.

Few of us are born storytellers. If we find ourselves frequently bored by those around it's a safe assumption that the reverse may also be true. Because developing a strong narrative drive is the most difficult, frequently painful aspect of writing, too little time is spent learning it. That is reason enough why so many so-called 'literary' writers derisively dismiss inspired storytelling as contrivance. This attitude is aided and abetted by those critics and teachers who continue to denigrate 'plot' as somehow unworthy, stating preferences for stories which are 'character driven.'

This is widely off the mark. It should be obvious that no story can work if it is **not** character driven.

Plot should never be—in fact **cannot** be—separated from character; plot is, after all, nothing less than what happens when a character—called the protagonist—is motivated to 'do', or 'get' something, then subsequently confronted with another character or characters motivated to prevent this doing or getting.

A lack of attention to character motivation, along with similar inattention to cause and effect (as in **domino effect**, a triggering incident causing other incidents to happen in turn), leads to a kind of vacuum, the major reason why so many books can be laid aside, never to be picked up again.

Like it or not, telling exciting, suspenseful stories is an essential part of the fictional art. Luckily, this too can be learned.

BEFORE CREATING THE NARRATIVE (STORY) LINE

Though taking the time to find out what it is about the notion or idea that is so attractive and compelling to you before beginning the actual work may seem like unnecessary delay, it will pay enormous dividends in the long run.

The choice is simple. You can write complete drafts of the work, making it up as you go along, with the immense expenditure of time and energy that exploring the material in this manner takes. Or you can write **about** the work, which is not only demonstrably more efficient, but produces a more focused and powerful story.

WRITE THE BOOKJACKET COPY

The easiest way to get started is to write a bookjacket of the novel (or blurb for the play or screenplay) you have in mind.

Examine the bookjackets of the books that you own. You do own many books, do you not? If you, as a would-be novelist, do not buy novels, how can you expect anyone to buy your books when they are published? Further, in order to keep the well of your subconscious full to brimming, you have to keep adding to it. The first three most important rules of learning how to write are (1) Write (2) Write and (3) Write. The next three are (4) Read (5) Read and (6) Read!

Look for those bookjackets that you think are most effective; those you remember impelling you to pick up the book in the first place. Now try to write a bookjacket that is similarly intriguing for the novel you have in mind. Be swift, be strong, be tantalizing, be brief.

Would your bookjacket synopsis cause a bookstore browser (based on someone much like yourself) to sample a few pages of your novel? If unsure, rewrite your bookjacket copy, keeping in mind the limitations of space, and put more punch into it. Do not shrink from enhancing (making melodramatic) the elements of your story, even if you have every intention of presenting them in a more subtle, sophisticated way later.

Think of the bookjacket copy as a kind of preview of coming attractions.

It would also help for you to think about what you

intend to say in your query letter to agents and editors. Will your presentation intrigue them enough to want to see your novel?

By putting an honest effort into singling out the key selling points (another way of saying entertainment values) of your novel, you will be focusing on your novel's strengths. Peel away any extraneous matters. Concentrate solely on your story's direction. In this way, you can proceed in a straight line to the heart (and soul) of the matter.

CREATING THE STORY LINE

Once you have created bookjacket copy which promises a reader all the passion and excitement you hope to pour into your novel, the next step is optional: you can either write a review (see below) of the novel (or play/screenplay) you're planning to write, or, if you feel confident that you now have a handle on just what your idea is, you can start reeling out the story line.

Perhaps the most effective, and certainly the most straightforward way to create a story line is simply to write down everything that is going to happen in your story sequentially.

Keep it simple. This is not the moment to be inventing byzantine structures. If you haven't been a reader of comic strips, this may be a good time to start. There's no better example of how to succinctly use narrative events with beginnings, middles and ends that result in satisfying denouements than comic strips. After all, isn't that the goal in a synopsis such as the one you're attempting to write?

Write fast.

You may be amazed at just how far into the narrative you may get before, as is inevitable, you bog down. If, or perhaps more accurately, when you stall, proper use of the SECRET STORY techniques should give you enough additional material to speed you on your way again.

Before sleep every night, keep putting the question to your subconscious: Dear Partner, What's going to happen next?

Additional scenes will multiply, not only those that take place in sequence after the spot where you bogged down, but some that take place before and in between those scenes that you have already written.

If you draw a blank; that is, if you reach a dead end, and can't seem to come up with a satisfying end to your story, pause and re-group. Put away the pages you have, let them (and you) marinate for, say, a week or more, so that you can re-read them with a fresh eye.

Now rephrase the question to your subconscious: Dear Partner, Have you told me everything that can possibly happen to these characters? And is it certain how they will end up?

If properly done, better gird yourself to cope with endings you wouldn't have dreamed of under ordinary circumstances.

Keep in mind that when you dramatize events, and when you explore the parameters of human behavior, you are, by definition, going beyond the ordinary. The hope, of course, is that in this process you will have created something extraordinary.

Be accepting, therefore, of whatever your subconscious throws up to you, no matter how surprising. Never dismiss any idea, no matter how seemingly outrageous. Instead, go back over the sequence of events and seek out whatever the logic might be for the surprises. Don't be afraid to shuffle the sequences, or to shift your characters in and out of the minor/major roles to see which of them might have the proper motivation.

Sooner or later, the inevitable question arises: When, you may well ask, will the point be reached where the actual writing of the novel itself can begin? One or several of the scenes that have surfaced will seem so exciting you will be tempted to abort this process and get to work on the actual manuscript immediately.

You will have difficulty resisting this siren's call. But do resist. You can relieve the pressure to dramatize by inserting bits of action and dialogue in the narrative synopsis. But instead of succumbing completely to the pleasures that writing the actual scene will give you, keep yourself on a leash. Frustrating or not, your job is to keep advancing the story line until you reach a satisfactory end. Time spent in this way avoids much more time wasted later. Otherwise, you may once again find yourself exploring situations which all too often turn into cul de sacs.

Be assured that when you do finally release yourself to write, all those repressed energies will come pouring out to reinvigorate the material, as well as the idea itself—and, not incidentally, the author.

Make no mistake about it: this is an agonizing process. It is the most difficult aspect of writing, and not for the faint of heart. But once embarked on the actual manuscript, you will find yourself as grateful as any well-trained athlete who spends much more time devoted to arduous, pre-event conditioning than to the actual event itself.

In the back of your mind during this preliminary period, you should remember to keep deciphering text. At all times try to remain aware that the writing process is a search for the thematic statement. Your job is to find out just what it is that your subconscious, through the story you are telling, is trying to say.

Do not become disheartened, however, if even after writing the narrative treatment, or synopsis, you're unable to boil the material down into a single, powerful theme. And do not allow yourself to be tempted into accepting the false luxury of several themes, deluding yourself that a multiplicity of themes indicates a certain profundity on the author's part. What you'll be doing is inviting incoherence, which will mislead and confuse any eventual reader.

Simplicity of theme does not mean weightlessness. Nor does it mean a lack of complexity. By not speaking out of both sides of your mouth at once, your reader learns to respect your authority, and you will have prevented deconstructionists, those enemies of attributable text, any opportunity to run amok.

When the subtextual message is clear and unadulterated and clearly focused, it takes on an irresistible power, meshing so inextricably with the whole it feels organic. The story will advance in a manner so seemingly inevitable it allows for no other choices.

MAKING SENSE OF (REVIEWING) THE STORY LINE

Congratulations! You've now written the equivalent of a narrative treatment, otherwise known as a synopsis, from beginning to end.

Having put your narrative away for a time you may notice upon rereading that, though vastly improved, it still doesn't seem all that powerful. Indeed, it may seem vague and slightly incoherent, not to mention undramatic. Your scenes seem to sprawl randomly; if there was a point you've forgotten it; your characters wander like underutilized actors in search of a drama in which they may act out their parts in a convincing manner.

But no doubt there are also scenes you do not even

recall writing about that now seem vivid and unconventional, and there are one or more characters that are so uniquely individual they surprise even you. (Let's hope one of them is the protagonist!)

List those key scenes, including startling moments; they are touchstones to the solving of any problems your narrative may have.

If you haven't felt the need to do so earlier, now may be the time to write a glowing review of the novel you have in mind.

Putting modesty aside, imagine that you are the leading reviewer of the most influential publication in the country, and are going to do your utmost to convince readers that they must go out and buy your novel immediately!

"Let's not mince words," you may write. "This is a stunning novel, written by (your name here), a master of his/her craft, who has produced an enthralling, and yes, profound work that keeps the reader engrossed from first page to last."

Okay so far: You've tantalized your audience. But in order to get them to rush out to the bookstore to buy your novel, you must first give them a reason, and that involves telling them who and what your book is about. Seems easy enough...

"The protagonist," you continue enthusiastically, "a person with a dominant attribute (i.e., ambitious young priest, melancholy Dane, faithless wife, greedy stock manipulator, frightened soldier), encounters another character with a dominant attribute (see examples above), who offers a fatal temptation. "In a momentary lapse, for reasons buried deep within his/her psyche, the protagonist steps from the straight and narrow and in a series of harrowing events discovers (blank) about life and (blank) about him/herself."

Pause a moment here. Have you found it easy to describe a dominant trait about each of your characters? If not, why not? Could it be they're not well enough defined, even in your own mind? If so, it's imperative for you to learn more about them.

Do a little creative snooping into each character's history. You may discover hidden motivations that can surprise you, that must surprise you before you can surprise your readers.

And how clearly have you been able to describe the basic conflict? How determined is your protagonist to achieve some goal? What, or who, stands in your protagonist's way? Does every character you've created contribute to the dramatic action? If not, what are they doing in your story?

If these questions prove difficult to answer, try listing all the emotional and historical baggage your leading characters carry. If you approach these lists in the proper manner (see SECRET STORY techniques above) you will find things you didn't expect. Treasure them. (Like objects made of gold, they come in handy during hard times.)

Now chart your main characters' emotional journeys from the beginning to the end of your novel. Examine the result: Do your leading characters grow and develop?

Remember our definition of story? Readers know they've been told a story if they recognize that a protagonist has changed, and/or has at the very least been enlightened in some important, revelatory way.

In every relationship story (is there any other kind?) the characters should change or enlighten each other.

Critics of the "I'll know what I like when I see it!" school, operating without any objective standard, or theory of drama by which to judge, are unable to identify for the reader why something in the fiction under consideration worked, or did not, except in the most general terms. A large metropolitan newspaper's influential film critic once actually complained, in a review, that characters in a film she disliked had caused changes in each other. The film might have esthetically failed for a number of reasons, but that was not one of them.

If characters in a story do not impact one another, then what are they doing in the story? Even a random encounter should have a reason for being; even casual 'walk-ons' should be placed there for effect. Otherwise an author is being careless, littering the narrative with material that is flawed. If an author cannot find a reason for it, reason enough to take it out.

What about the dramatic action?

As you continue writing your review, do you find it easy to sketch the narrative line (sometimes called plot) in a gripping way, yet clearly enough for a reasonably intelligent person to understand it? (Try explaining your story to someone other than another writer. If your listener can't grasp what's going on in your story, there's little doubt it's not sufficiently focused.)

CHOOSING (IDENTIFYING) THE PROTAGONIST

Choosing—or, more accurately, being chosen by a protagonist—is probably the most important decision a writer will make. It is not as easy as it might seem. If an author knows that a character is going to change, or by story's end will have an epiphanic insight into self, that character is clearly identified as protagonist.

If, however, near a story's end, a subsidiary character suddenly steps forward and takes over the action, it is a strong signal for the author to examine whether the original choice was correct.

In many cases, the potential for failure lies elsewhere. In the years that I have been conducting workshops and seminars, it amazes me how often writers offer up protagonists who do not act but are instead acted upon, or are protagonists who, if not victimized by others, are merely passive observers of the passing scene.

More years ago than I like to remember, my literary agent, Don Congdon, cautioned me that since writers are by occupation sedentary, and sedentary occupations lead its practitioners to become passive, they tend to create passive protagonists.

This rarely results in anything good; most often, what happens—or more accurately, what does not happen—can be summed up in a single word: borrrrringggg!

Obviously a passive protagonist is not much help in pushing a story along.

A late, great writing teacher, in commenting upon the slices of life sketches then, as more infrequently now, fashionable in *New Yorker* fiction, observed that one way to know if a story's been told is to see if the protagonist changes at the end. (In a relationship story, I'd add, the characters ought to change one another.)

Unless the point of a story is precisely that no matter what happens to a protagonist there will never be change, an aramadillo nature deflecting all assaults, a change in a character's attitude—or sudden insight into self—provides the simplest test that what's been written can be identified as a story.

If it's not a story, it may be many things, some even good, but what ought to be a fiction writer's primary goal hasn't been accomplished: to wit, taking a reader on a journey all the way through to emotional release, what the Greeks called catharsis.

CARING ABOUT THE PROTAGONIST

Should your protagonist be sympathetic?

Not necessarily, though no doubt a story with sympathetic characters has a better chance of finding publication.

Again, in thinking about creating sympathetic protagonists, look to our simplest art forms.

Originally, in Western movies, black hats and white hats identified villains and heroes. As they became more sophisticated, other techniques were used. Barnaby Conrad, working writer and artist, head of the Santa Barbara Writers Conference, has talked about 'kick the dog Westerns', where audiences immediately recognized the bad guys because of their behavior.

Similarly, the heroes, no matter how long or arduous their ride, always took care of their horses before going into the saloon to slake their own thirst. Villains, however, jumped off the poor beasts whose heaving flanks were foamed with sweat and with the fillip of an additional kick or a curse strode inside and raucously demanded "Whiskey, leave the bottle!"

If unsure whether the protagonist you've created will be perceived sympathetically by the reader, it's simple enough to have them provide a simple act of kindness for beast, or man.

But it's not sympathy alone that moves audiences, it's understanding. Leslie Abramson, defense attorney for two acknowledged parricides, the Menendez brothers, got enough of the jury to buy into the purported reasons which drove her clients to kill their parents, alleging physical and sexual abuse, to cause a hung jury. (Which led to the joke about the murderers pleading for mercy on the grounds that they were orphans.)

Even with characters more sympathetic than these, an audience will still seek understanding, though the writer's job is much easier.

But the most unsavory character can be sympathized with, even if disliked, as long as we learn how that character was formed. In the unsuccessful film, *W.C. Fields & Me*, W.C. Fields abuses his mistress, Carlotta, physically and emotionally.

Understandably, we don't like him. Unfortunately, we've also been programmed not to like the film about him either, an unconscious but unmistakable signal to dislike transmitted to the audience through the symbol of an incontinent dog. (More about Fields and the film, later.)

Another example is the running gag throughout Robert Altman's ill-fated film, (*Pret a porter*) *Ready to Wear*, in which the toilet habit of dogs tells us all too graphically how Altman felt about his subject matter.

Obviously, it helps to create both sympathy and understanding if the characters being written about are people the writer finds compelling, and not contemptible.

If for some reason you set out to tell a story about a boring character, you've given yourself a daunting, though not necessarily an impossible task. What you mustn't do, of course, is write about that character in a boring way.

Is your character aware that he's boring? If he is, and can't help himself, we may pity and even admire him—as long as he fights to overcome his boringness. We can appreciate his efforts, even in a losing cause. Make this character self-pitying, however, and what readers will feel is annoyance and contempt. We admire those who want to better themselves. It gives us an excuse to 'root for' the protago-nist.

It may also be wise to test your own capacity for boring others by observing the reactions you provoke amongst your own social circle. If your friends' eyes glaze over when you talk, it's fair to assume you're not a spell-binder. (If your own eyes glaze over, imagine how your audience feels!)

Another worthwhile test is to read your stories aloud to a group. Nothing makes a writer as intensely con-scious of long-windedness and irrelevant discursiveness as becoming aware of a restless stirring and clearing of throats during the reading of one's own work.

ORGANIZING THE MATERIAL: STRENGTHENING A STORY'S BONES

If the story line—even in an episodic, metaphorical novel—does not possess some kind of interior logic, or if the events, sparse as they may be, only 'happen' randomly, without motivation save for the author's recognition of the need for some kind of 'action', it is probably necessary to take a more practical, hands-on approach to organizing the material.

Creating order out of chaos has been rightfully termed the artist's primary job. More good ideas for stories fail because the author has failed to get a 'handle' on the material.

Developing a structure that will keep a story within pre-set boundaries may be anathema to free versifiers and writers who prefer to be guided solely by inspiration, but it is absolutely essential for those authors who wish to wring every emotional drop out of the material at hand.

Storytelling without structure is like playing tennis

without a net: boring to all, and especially to spectators.

Paradoxically, the more a story can be kept within bounds, the more inventive the author can become.

Once the guideposts are in place, the author's concentration is no longer confined to the task of searching for ways to advance the story; instead of stumbling along unfamiliar terrain, s/he may give full concentration to details, and can be as inventive in character and event as talent will allow.

The simplest way to structure a story is arbitrarily to break the material into three acts. (It may be a story of many acts, unnatural and otherwise, but for the purpose of this discussion, assume there are only three.)

Act I—state the situation, or provide the hook, or write what in other words is known as the inciting incident.

Act II—complicate the situation.

Act III—resolve the situation.

What could be easier?

Act II, traditionally the *bête noire* of all writers, can be overcome by searching the text to find a major complication.

At the end of Act I, with a complication introduced, the story is not only launched headlong into Act II, but most importantly, it brings the audience hastening back after intermission.

If you're not writing a story of suspense, perhaps you should be. In any (make that every) case, it's appropriate to borrow from the genre.

All stories should be suspenseful.

If suspense has not been created, everything after the inciting incident, no matter how beautifully written, begins to seem overwrought and tedious.

If all else fails, think betrayal.

Writers, locked inside their own minds so much of the time, are luckily prone to paranoia. Writers can, and should use this aberrant view to look for possibilities of betrayal in the characters they're writing about.

Example: a trusted friend, or lover, say, of the protagonist, who at the end of Act I is suddenly, and surprisingly, revealed to be an antagonist, is a complication that reinforces suspense, and brings the audience hastening back for Act II, or a reader, long past sleep time, happily turning the pages to see what's going to happen next.

In this example, the end of Act II can then be similarly enhanced by having the protagonist suddenly made aware that the person previously thought of as friend/lover is actually a betrayer, and we rush back for Act III, or turn the pages for the next chapter, anxious to see how this conflict will be resolved.

Within each act of a play, of course, are scenes. If you are writing a novel, think instead of chapters.

Arbitrarily, think of the novel you're going to write as containing, say, sixteen chapters (in order not to be overly symmetrical). Now place the chapters, or scenes, where they seem most to belong within the act structure.

Five (or six) scenes that help state the situation, or problem, belong in Act I. Five (or six) that complicate the situation are listed in Act II. And the remaining scenes that are needed to resolve the problem will naturally be placed in Act III.

Don't worry if you can't think of what might happen in chapters two, three or four, to fill out the first act. Leave them blank. (You can certainly come up with the opening chapter, and the complicating chapter that ends Act I, so all that's left to think up are two or three others.)

Proceed in a similar manner to describe the scenes,

or chapter headings, of Act II, and, similarly, those of Act III.

In the chapters noted that are not blank, there will be clues to dramatic happenings, past and future. Use the SECRET STORY techniques to ferret them out.

Remember, every night before sleep, to ask your subconscious for help. Remember to decipher your text by using your own key words and phrases to trigger ideas.

Remember also premonitions. And remember that the behavior of your characters at the end of the novel needs to have been foreshadowed in the beginnings.

A lack of **foreshadowings** make endings arbitrary and abrupt because they lack motivational context. Arbitrary, or ambiguous endings are the refuge of the artistically impoverished.

By working forward and back in this manner, the blank chapters will soon be filled in, and your story will have a strong chance of achieving its maximum artistic potential.

THE STORY 'HOOK'

A story hook is exactly what the term implies—a narrative device so powerful readers are 'hooked', and will keep turning pages long after the first encounter.

Merely describing an action scene, even one as violent as an act of rape or murder or general mayhem, seldom keeps us ensnared for the long haul.

In order for readers to care about what happens to the person at risk they must first know enough about the potential victim to feel sympathetic. This does not mean there is a need for exposition, or a lengthy rundown of background information, but simply to provide enough clues as to dominant characteristics that will, in effect, put flesh on what would otherwise be a stick–figure character.

Alert readers of the paragraph above will have noted the words **at risk** and **potential** and **dominant characteristic**.

Setting a scene that is ominous and full of foreboding is much more gripping than a willy–nilly plunge into a violent act.

Example: a hospital entrance with its nighttime comings and goings can be observed from the point of view of someone unknown (silent observers are almost always perceived as threatening) watching and evaluating (for purposes we can reasonably assume are dire) a shift of nurses going off duty. Inside, a night nurse on her way out stops to care for a needy patient, establishing her character as nurturing (not a surprise, but comforting.) By the time the nurse heads for the parking lot or bus stop she's alone—except, of course, for the ominous secret observer.

MAD Magazine, years ago, had a series of spoofs about Hollywood movies titled *And you know WHO gets killed!* Prime example: a squad of soldiers pauses for a water break; wallets are produced; a young soldier passes around photos of his wife and newborn child. The caption: *And you know WHO gets killed!* Or the pilot volunteering for that one last mission before returning home: (*A-y-k-W-g-k!*) Or a character threatening to inform the authorities: (*A-y-k-W-g-k!*) etc.

A victim's humanity has to be established before an audience can identify enough to care. Case in point, from a personal experience: when in the Pacific during World War II my Army outfit, in our first combat invasion, waded ashore a coral atoll, passing a number of Japanese dead from the preliminary bombardment. None of us were demonstrably upset—until we encountered our first dead

Americans. Immediately identifying with our own kind, we became near overwhelmed by an abiding self-concern (a condition more widely known as fear.)

My erstwhile partner in advertising, Robert Weverka, with whom, as an experiment, I wrote a novel, (*The Widowmaster*/Fawcett Gold Medal) used to point out that pulp fiction provided a unique primer in how to write openings that would absolutely hook a reader.

Example, in the Western genre: "The cowboy shifted in the saddle and looked down upon the herd of cattle he intended to rustle that night. Meanwhile, back at the ranch, the pretty daughter of the spread's ailing owner, whose arthritis had flared with the approaching storm, encouraged him to stay in bed. "You stay put, daddy dear," she told him, "I'll saddle Old Satan and ride out to calm the herd."

Of course, the main rule in writing is to do whatever works.

In Elmore Leonard's *Unknown Man Number 89*, the author seems to spend an inordinate number of pages not doing much more than describing a character. But what description! The manner in which that character is described lets us know that he's someone bound to get into trouble, sooner rather than later.

STRUCTURING STORIES FOR MAXIMUM SUSPENSE

Always leave your audiences wanting more.

The late, lamented Hugh (Timmy) Brooke, British novelist and playwright, once considered the peer of Evelyn Waugh and Graham Greene (and, according to actress Lauren Bacall, responsible for her entry into show business), used to attempt, as a writing exercise, to come up with miniature cliffhangers at the bottom of every page, hoping to make it impossible for readers not to turn that page.

A best-selling novelist I know, in the early stages of her career, used to enlarge margins, side to side, top and bottom, in the hopes that editors would exclaim, as manuscript pages whipped by, "Whatever else, this book is certainly a page-turner!"

That may be taking the issue of suspense a bit far afield; conceptually, however, it's the kind of narrative pull writers should always be attempting to achieve with their work.

As a matter of craft, not only every piece of fiction, but indeed, every piece of writing, should contain all the elements of suspense, from hooking the reader at the beginning through several twists and turns all the way to the surprising (but satisfactory) climax at the end.

This does not mean arbitrarily withholding information, a tactic revelatory of the amateur who in this manner creates a mystery which is false and off-putting.

MYSTERY VS. SUSPENSE

Mystery and suspense are closely allied, which is perhaps why the publishing industry continues to use the misleading catchall term "Mystery" to identify both.

But there's a difference between mystery and suspense.

Mystery is a puzzle: solving what has happened.

Suspense is a state of mind: apprehension, or excited anticipation, over what's about to happen.

There is very little action in a mystery. In a mystery, whatever violence there is has usually taken place before the story begins.

In suspense, there is much more action and less mystery, with the protagonist under constant threat of attack and/or continually having to surmount dangerous obstacles.

There can be mystery in a suspense story, though there does not have to be. The same is true, vice versa, in the mystery.

The most powerful form of suspense is when the audience knows something the protagonist does not.

This can be seen in a simple situation: a character about to walk through a door behind which lurks a character with evil intent.

Mysteries are whodunits. In suspense we know the who, what we're trying to discover is why.

Suspense can be achieved by stating a protagonist's goal (see 'Cowboy shifting in saddle' above), and then following the story to see how, or whether, the goal is achieved.

In *Sunset Boulevard*, as in *Betrayal*, the procedure is reversed: we begin at the end, and avidly follow along to see why and how the narrator wound up dead in the swimming pool.

The mystery in suspense stories is usually whether and how something succeeds. There is also the why of motivation. We read not only to find out what happens, but to find out why.

In *Betrayal*, we watch the developing love affair with mounting dismay, having already been made aware it is coming to no good end. And we avidly seek out clues that would have foretold the death of the affair.

Keep in mind that withholding information from the reader creates artificial suspense and risks alienating readers; withholding knowledge from the character, but informing the reader, enhances suspense, and makes a friend of the reader.

A good rule of thumb for an author in any kind of fiction (or, indeed, any kind of narrative) is never to give away more information than is necessary to keep advancing the story. Any explaining is done through the characters, who will provide information when another character has need of it. Usually one or both characters should be in a highly emotional state, the kind that lead to revelations.

III

STORYTELLING TECHNIQUES
& DEVICES

WHERE DOES THE STORY BEGIN?

Where to start?

During a recent tenure as chairman of a large writer's organization fiction awards committee, I read more than one hundred and fifty published works of fiction, and found it remarkable how many writers (and, clearly, their editors) flunked this most obvious of questions. Most of the stories started everywhere except where they ought, (which is at the beginning, of course.)

But like all speakers (and writing in this sense can be said to be comparable to written-down talk) writers commonly warm up first by throat (mind) clearings. Rather than conducting this ritual off stage, before actually stepping forward to perform, however, too many writers warm up center stage. This tendency is easily dealt with by curtaining off (eliminating) first paragraphs, pages, and even, more often than not, chapters. Try starting later, see if what's eliminated was actually necessary or was instead useless clutter.

The second biggest mistake writers make, next to believing action is sure-fire reader ensnarement, is not only to produce a surfeit of background explanation before the story has started but every time a character is introduced.

Exposition has no place anywhere in storytelling.

An author's urge to explain is a danger signal, a warning that the author's agenda has taken priority over character agendas.

An author explaining anything virtually guarantees reader boredom.

How then does an author convey information? By letting the drama do the job. Sooner or later the story's characters will demand and convey information, one to and from another, for manipulative purposes of their own. (See section on exposition, below, for further details.)

Where the story actually begins can be recognized when an action (or lack of an action) by some *who* initiates (or permits) a chain of events (the *what*) to take place.

The vastly underrated John O'Hara's *Appointment in Samarra*, (whose theme is stated up front by the parable from which O'Hara took his title) is a classic example. The protagonist, Julian English, walks into his country club's locker room and throws his drink in another member's face. What follows is the story of Julian's inevitable disintegration.

The parable? A man hears Death is looking for him in Samarkand, hastily flees to Samarra, where to his surprise he encounters Death, who expresses delight, because his earlier schedule had been changed.

Instead of thinking hook, writers might better think of beginnings as similar to lighting a fuse or igniting a trail of gunpowder that will eventually result in an explosion.

Or, for those with a gentler bent, a beginning might be compared to the tipping of the first domino in a lengthy row.

Those who insist, however, that no story works where context is not developed get no argument from me. But context will become apparent when characters pursue goals and conflict one with another, expressing emotion through thought and action.

This works particularly well if the context, part of which is the physical environment, is described in terms that reflect the emotional outlook of the characters. Revealed in this manner, bit by bit, context becomes part of the overall suspense.

Background is no more context (unless in flashback or prologue) than a character resume is characterization. Behavior, emotionally felt thought and motivated action define character. Exposition must never, repeat never, be used before stories begin.

If, however, an author continues to feel that the story s/he wants to tell will only be effective after the reader is told the character histories or how the situation those characters find themselves in has developed, then a **prologue** or **flashback** (discussed later in these pages) should be considered as an option.

Of course if a writer is clever enough, other options can be utilized. In Harold Pinter's film *Betrayal* (adapted from a play by the author), for example, the action begins with the breakup of an affair, and the story thereafter unreels backward, finally ending with the beginning of the relationship (of which more later.)

In all such cases the primary rule, **Whatever Works**, has to apply.

PROLOGUES, THEIR USES AND FUNCTIONS

By definition, prologue is what has taken place before the story begins.

Prologue is history.

Is the story a hunt for buried treasure? A prologue can show how the treasure was created, or how it happened to be buried: for instance, the sinking of the Spanish galleon loaded with doubloons. Or villains—or refugees—might stash cash in a nearly inaccessible hiding place. Or it may be the collapse of an ancient Incan mine, covering all traces of the riches to be found there. Even the creation of the earth or the forming of a river might be described, should this have a bearing on the story to be told.

Think how effective the prologue is of William Peter Blatty's *The Exorcist*. An anthropological dig, cracking open the earth's crust, releases demons into the world. Chapter one (the beginning of the actual story) opens with the priest/protagonist (whom the title identifies) being called in to deal with the possessed girl.

A reader will more likely believe an amulet to have magic powers if shown how that amulet was created and who put the magic into it. A genie will seem more real if we see how the genie came into being, or came to be stuffed into the bottle.

A prologue serves then either as a metaphor, or as a background against which the story plays out. Sometimes it is both metaphor and context. What a prologue is not is the story itself.

The traditional well-made play, at curtain's rise, usually had butler and maid, while dusting the room or preparing table for the upcoming dinner party speaking dialogue like: "Does Master know that Madame has been consulting with that young rogue, Fortescue?" This served as a kind of prologue, setting up the situation, while at the same time providing an explanation of the story's context; but the main business of the play, which is story, did not begin until Master and Madame entered.

Setting up a 'frame', or 'book-end' for a story that will be told in flashback, is, strictly speaking, not prologue. But it serves a similar function. (For more on how to 'frame' stories, see STRUCTURE, above.)

POINTS OF VIEW

Arguably, the easiest way to tell a story is to use the omniscient point of view.

Yet many writers (including this one) are drawn toward the artistic challenge of telling stories in the first person. And it is a challenge, make no mistake about that.

Unfortunately, when writers are in the early stages of their careers, their skills are understandably limited. They may be unaware of the pitfalls they may encounter because they've limited themselves to the narrative eye (sic.)

Or, when the "I" is more "I" than eye, what writers frequently forget is that the "I" is a character separate from the author, and must be described, both inside and out.

Because there is an "I" telling the story does not make this requirement less essential. Too often, writers forget that the "I" does not refer to themselves, but to another that they have created.

Even if a supposedly fictional story is more or less autobiographical, an author should never assume his audience will take him at face value (otherwise why tell the story?) Writing about a character in the third person, on the other hand, forces the author to describe that character both as to physical attributes and emotional attitudes.

Other difficulties afflict the "I". The author is locked into a singular point of view. If, some distance into the work, upon a sudden perceived need to present the viewpoint of other characters, the author switches to third person, this alienates the reader. Upon becoming aware, consciously or unconsciously, how illogical (not to mention inartistic) the author's conception is, the reader loses faith in the storyteller. Like infidelity, it's a breach of an implied contract; though it may be forgiven, it's never forgotten.

In skilled hands, of course, there are ways around this. In Robert Penn Warren's masterpiece, *All the King's Men* (a novel in which every fictional device any writer might want can be found) though the entire story is told in the first person, Warren is always able to thrust his readers into a third person scene by some such deceptively simple device as having his narrator say something like, "I could imagine how Willie (the protagonist) must have taken the news. Waiting anxiously in his overheated room, the wood stove glowing cherry-red, Willie rushed to answer the frantic knock on his door..."

Equally restrictive is to tell the story from a single character's point of view. Starting a story from inside a character's head creates problems. Once a reader is locked inside a character's mind, it becomes damnably difficult to get out of that mind into another. A switch to another character's p.o.v. becomes jarring.

Why not instead, as Hemingway suggested, "tell them how the weather was?"

By describing the surroundings at a story's start, the reader (and author) are reminded that character and author are not one and the same; indeed, that an author exists.

Using the omnipotent point of view, which has countless advantages, need not intimidate writers. Once the pattern is established that there is an author, it will seem natural for that author to switch from one character to another without confusing the reader—as long as the author keeps in mind that not only should each character have an attitude, as Elmore Leonard commented during a visit to my workshop, but so, I add, should the author.

How the author feels about his or her characters will become evident from the tone in which the story is told—sardonic, amused, ironic or sympathetic (and not, as is too frequently the case from writers early in their careers, with a pseudo-objectivity, which can be deadly.) By setting a definite tone, and establishing a pattern, an author takes charge, creating an air of authority which puts the reader at ease. (It helps in accomplishing this if the author works hard at knowing everything there is to know about storyline and characters before the actual storytelling begins—about which more later.)

If an author prefers many individual voices telling a story, it's absolutely necessary for a pattern to be established. Typography can be useful here—heading each chapter with the name of the character speaking, thus implying (foreshadowing) that in succeeding chapters there will be other voices.

Before switching viewpoints, a useful way to underscore the transition is to have one character either discuss or think about the next character to be heard from. To make it easier, think of it as passing a baton in a relay.

When telling a story in 'voices' what is absolutely essential also is to particularize each voice, taking care to avoid coloring those voices with the inflections and cadences of their creator.

Whatever the technique chosen, and whatever the pattern established, it is essential not to deviate from it. I have always found it intolerable to lose myself reading a first person narrative, only to have it suddenly switched to third and back again for no reason easily discernible, which makes it seem to have been done solely for the author's (or the director's) convenience.

A writer should never take the reader out of the story, nor make him overly aware of the techniques involved.

It can't be said too often: the reader's priorities come first.

Character agendas must always come before those of the author.

Whenever an author feels the need to explain, bad things (loss of momentum, if not absolute tedium) result. Whenever a character feels the need to explain, however, that serves a function in the story. Following this dictum would eliminate most exposition, so as not to put a brake, sometimes permanent, on a reader's attention.

It is the author's, not the reader's job to make order out of chaos (unless the author is a sadist writing for masochists.) And the less aware a reader is of devices an author uses, the less likely the reader will become angered or frustrated enough to opt out of the story.

In my experience, authors who have little faith in the story they're telling tend to create overelaborate structures.

Authors who feel the necessity for exposition are revealing a similar lack of faith in their readers' intuitive and deductive powers.

When an author knows everything it is possible to know about where the story is going, and understands what each character's feelings are at every and any given point, the reader will intuit what is going on emotionally, and will happily fill in any gaps through deduction.

CHARACTER MOTIVATION

Some years ago, at a writers' conference, I attended a lecture given by a television hyphenate: that is, a writer-development executive.

The lecture, which dealt primarily with doing character biographies, was splendid: well-delivered, thoughtful—and significantly wrong. What the hyphenate proposed, as typical of how TV writers work, was that writers develop biographies of the main characters before using those characters in a story.

But this method ignores one of the joys—as well as the major connection linking conscious and subconscious—that the writing process provides. A great many writers, including myself, tell how it is precisely when a story's characters take on a life of their own that gives the best indication that a story is working.

KEEP A CONTINUING BIOGRAPHY

Instead, what a writer should do is brainstorm about the characters, using the same techniques as are used in brainstorming story (see SECRET STORY above.)

Try not to limit character choices. Giving characters their heads, letting them do what they may, opens up many opportunities for unpredictable behavior.

When a character suddenly does something surprising, a writer should pause, celebrate (a character's action surprising the author will undoubtedly surprise the reader, in both cases a condition devoutly to be wished) and only then think about what would motivate that character to act in such a surprising way. In other words, an attempt should be made by the writer to discover whatever it is in the character's past that would foreshadow such an action. At that point, the writer can add to this character's biography in the certainty that the history will ring true.

As good a film as Calder Willingham's *The Graduate* was, the author missed a bet in not foreshadowing that this shy, repressed protagonist could, of a sudden, in contradiction to all expectations, step into a phone booth to call the voracious Mrs. Robinson. It would have taken only the briefest of moments, during the graduation party, say, for the Graduate to surreptitiously react, by some action (hidden from all but the audience) to the plethora of advice he was getting, thus establishing the possibility that he was capable of more than we were seeing. We'd still be surprised, but not bewildered, or unaccepting.

Audiences are very forgiving, more than willing to suspend disbelief, but they do not take the abuse of their patience lightly. The more a character's behavior is grounded in emotional logic, the more accepting an audience will be.

On that note, a shalt not: writers should never look to psychologists to 'vet' characters, or ask in any way for help in their creations.

Freud read Dostoevsky, Dostoevsky wrote without benefit of having read Freud.

Remember, within every author resides a complete range of human emotions, providing limitless possibilities for behavior. When writers become 'free' enough, in dialogues with their own subconsciousnesses, to give characters their heads, those characters, reflecting the authors who create them, reveal unique and individual behavior traits.

THE EMOTIONAL ARC

Probably the most important reminder for a writer—and one that should be hanging up in large capital letters over his or her writing place—is the word E-M-O-T-I-O-N!

No character enters a scene without feeling something. There is always anticipation or dread or various gradations thereof. Even those who approach a place or situation without expectation, in a state of doldrummery, will soon be surprised. (Or should be.)

Nor does anyone arrive on scene without an emotional history. Even a newly born babe has been conceived in some kind of passionate state, and carried to term in a variety of others. By the time years have been added to the mix, a character can be guaranteed to have experienced (or endured) the kind of emotional bombardment that make the barrages of modern warfare seem puny by comparison. An important source of conflict is the battle, inner or outer, that is continually being waged.

A character's emotional arc is a term that grew out of 'pitch' meetings in the film industry, in which development executives demand details about a character's emotional journey, from start to finish; i.e., what a character's attitude is at the beginning, and how is it different (or changed) by the end.

Because films are not usually made in sequence: i.e., scenes that take place in one location are grouped together, no matter when they supposedly take place, to simplify logistics, actors must be aware of the emotional 'place' their characters are in at various specific 'times' in order for their emotions to fit the particular scene.

Writers can borrow from the techniques of how actors work, and, in similar fashion, can ask themselves just what emotional state their characters are supposed to be in at any given moment. (It's always interesting, and valuable, for writers to get to know actors. Writers should ask themselves, when creating a character, how they would feel if asked to portray that character in an adaptation. Is there enough 'attitude' for the actor to get a 'handle' on the character?)

In the first draft, an author should never worry about larding his scenes with an excess of emotion. Overstating what the characters are feeling is better than leaving the matter in doubt. Excess, in the final polishings, is more easily trimmed back than trying to add emotions later.

For writers who have difficulty revealing emotion (either their own or their characters'), it might help to think in terms of grand or soap opera or melodrama. Almost every person's life is a soap opera, at least within their own minds.

In terms of the overall arc, however, writers, like actors, should keep in mind that starting at a feverishly high pitch leaves little room to go higher. No emotional high can be sustained for long, never mind over the course of a long journey. Lows as well as highs occur in every drama, however conflicted, as well as in life.

Quiet moments in narratives serve other functions as well: they not only set off subsequent high points, making such seem even more intense by comparison, but give readers as well as protagonists time to regroup. For example, moments in which characters falsely imagine themselves free of arduous situations create opportunities to take character, reader, and even, perhaps, the author, by surprise.

In classical drama, climaxes are always followed by a dying fall.

Contemporary fiction writers could do worse than hark back to the classics when looking for examples to emulate. Ray Bradbury has also advised writers to find a book they admire, one most like the book they are trying to write, and keep it as a touchstone to which they may refer whenever they run into problems during the writing of **their** book.

EXPOSITION, WHEN TO USE

In the best of all possible fiction, exposition is never

used. Explanation tends to smother suspense. An author should at all times try to quell any urge to explain anything to the reader about what is going on. An author's craft deals only with emotion and motivation and burgeoning events.

Authors who know everything there is to know about the story they are going to tell, including everything about the characters in that story, have no need to use exposition. If an author knows all, the reader will intuit it from the happenings in the drama. (See BEFORE CREATING THE NARRATIVE (STORY) LINE, above.)

Learn to trust the audience. In spite of H.L. Mencken's frequently tested assertion that "no one ever went broke underestimating the intelligence of the American public", Mencken overstated the point. He confused audience forbearance—their willing suspension of disbelief—with stupidity; a more likely explanation for the success of less than esthetically pleasing material is the near insatiable need of audiences for story!

If literarily inclined writers spent as much time on developing story as they do on achieving style—if they were rather to remind themselves that before writers can perform they must compose—they would attract a far greater, and far more enthusiastic audience.

In film, a sure sign that producers, witting or not followers of Mencken, distrust their audience's comprehension is their imposition of a voice over narration. They over explain what should be obvious from what they have chosen to put on the film.

Through a fluke, I attended a preview screening of Stephen Crane's *The Red Badge of Courage*. The film had no narration, and the story was perfectly clear. Later, I saw the narrated version (the only one, to my knowledge, available today) and saw how leaden a device the voice over narration was.

Except as a deliberately startling device, such as the dead man in the Hollywood swimming pool who narrates Charles Brackett's & Billy Wilder's *Sunset Boulevard*, a voice over narration is almost always an admission by the film-makers that they themselves have failed to convey their film's content or meaning.

But paper is cheaper than film. Time spent re-working scripts is less costly than time spent re-shooting scenes.

A great director and great actors cannot save a bad script; a bad director, and bad acting, cannot completely ruin a great one.

I once saw Arthur Miller's play *The Crucible* per-formed by amateurs in a stuffy church basement—in spite of far less than perfect conditions, that production was enormously effective, moving some in the audience to tears.

The film industry might take a lesson from advertis-ing (or from these pages): concept dictates content, the sub-stance of that content dictates style. Those incapable of understanding this will produce unsuccessful films more often than not, and, of a certainty, produce films not nearly as successful as they ought to be.

EXPOSITION AVOIDANCE TECHNIQUES

An exercise in exposition avoidance for writers: imagine two characters, each desperately in love with the other, each determined never to reveal the felt love until the other declares love first. The two characters can talk about everything or anything under the sun but the love each feels for the other and it is a near guarantee that the audience will intuit what is going on, and will have a good time in the bargain.

Think about the process we undergo when encountering strangers, particularly attractive ones. How avidly we observe mannerisms; how we seize upon casual hints as to background and personality, putting together a mosaic of clues that will gradually form a picture of just what sort of character it is we're confronted with.

It's suspenseful, and it's fun. Why not provide your readers similar enjoyment?

To do this effectively, however, it is absolutely of first importance for the author to explore everything they think and feel about the story they plan to write before charging off on the writing of the actual manuscript, using the techniques above (see SECRET STORY), and below.

THE NECESSITY OF FORESHADOWING

In order for the reader not to feel cheated, foreshadowing is essential, not only in suspense and mystery writing, but in all fiction as well.

In good storytelling, an author must always—yes, always—drop hints and clues about character motivation, using gestures and slips of the tongue, portents and omens, as to what incidents will eventually take place.

This does not mean giving the mystery away; what it does mean is that the author is honor bound not to frustrate the reader by withholding information, or to cheat by deliberate misdirection. 'Red herrings' are never an acceptable device.

In a murder mystery, for example, we have seen how good writers never resort to misleading their readers, and neither should authors of 'serious' fiction.

On a subliminal level a reader, even if so caught up in the events s/he is unwilling to stop reading long enough to predict what finally happens at the end, will, upon reflection, realize that the 'clues' had been there all along, and winds up doubly satisfied because the author has played fair.

What has happened is that before writing the final draft, authors, having learned everything there is to know about every aspect of their stories, write with the full participation of their creative partners, the subconscious. As a result, the subtext beneath what the characters do and say takes on a potency that seeps directly into the reader's consciousness, thus increasing the emotional content of the story, thereby not only enhancing the reader's understanding, but his I.Q. (Identification Quotient) as well.

REWRITING

Some writers boast that they've never had to rewrite, apparently believing the work to have sprung fully-formed from their (Olympian) brows.

Other writers, Hemingway foremost among them, insist that it is rewriting that separates the men from the boys. In this equal opportunity age, let's instead say rewriting differentiates the professional from the amateur.

I couldn't agree more. Instead of being looked upon as loathsome drudgery, rewriting should be approached as an unequalled opportunity to make the work better.

How to start?

By resting.

That is, put the work aside, allowing it to marinate for a while, while you divert your mind with other, less arduous entertainments. Only then, after making sure you have allowed yourself sufficient time, read it in one fell swoop, continuously from start to finish, trying to take the material by surprise (or, what is more desirable, to be taken by surprise.)

If you are not one of those writers whose every

word seems permanently written in stone, the virtue of objectivity has been added to your arsenal.

What you're reading for mainly is story continuity, along with remaining alert for any slackening in the dramatic tension.

Do not stop mid-read to make changes. At the most, note wherever a story glitch or character anomaly, or, most important of all, a lack of tension, occurs.

If you find yourself drowsing over the pages, be assured the reader will also.

There are writers, on the other hand, whose first instinct is to cut—an excellent strategy. A vigorous weeding of the material certainly allows the prose garden you have created to breathe, so that its main ideas, like well-nurtured plants, stand revealed in all their naked glory.

Other writers, usually after receiving critiques which raise questions of puzzlement or curiosity, add material.

Inserting material into the text can cause another, more pernicious problem. Though it is natural for writers to trust in the power of language, the naive belief that by adding a few adjectives or a sentence hither and yon they have 'fixed' a misconception about a character or a story line never fails to astonish me.

It is unlikely that such minimal work, even if, or especially if **woven** (a literary conceit of many writers) throughout the manuscript, will have enough impact on the reader to produce the desired effect.

Instead, writers would be well-advised to find places in the text which allow for operatic, or Shakespearean 'moments'; that is, soliloquies or other character declamations, after which a story situation or a character's state of mind will be so firmly established there can be no questions about either.

It is also essential to keep in mind that any change or addition, from words to scene switchings, calls for the writer to reexamine, if not actually to rewrite, every word that precedes or follows the change.

Unlike the days of paste-pot and shears, computers have made it so relatively simple for writers to rearrange their material—little fuss, no muss—that it is often forgotten how the right words spoken in one situation can so easily become wrong when spoken in another. Even the slightest change in sequence can affect the tone, as well as the meaning, of everything which follows.

While it is excellent training for writers, in order to keep their minds agile, to think constantly on how to restructure everything, from scenes to complete acts, every shift should be evaluated to make certain the intended effect has been created, or if not, to be prepared to take the story into a new direction.

I was once hired by CBS to write an original teleplay—a so-called "docudrama"—about a real-life white middle-class doctor who conducted his practice in a gang-ridden ghetto. After following him about his daily rounds for a few weeks, I began writing the treatment.

From the project's inception, the producer, a former game show host, called me daily with "ideas" for the drama. When I was finally fully embarked upon my story 'treatment', I told him that I was no longer able to entertain any more suggestions from him. Furious, he demanded to know why. "Because," I replied, "I'm in the midst of my juggling act—that is, I've got all my story balls in the air, and if you continue to toss additional balls into the mix I'm certain to lose my concentration. When I've finished the treatment, and you read what I've done, we can discuss whether your additional ideas fit."

I had failed to make him understand the writer's mind, and the project was soon abandoned.

At some point, the rewrite of a manuscript should be a page one rewrite. That is, start back at the very beginning, word one, and at least look at every word and sentence, putting it through the computer of your mind, to make certain of its emotional, as well as sequential, appropriateness.

Whatever your situation, *do not despair.* Even in the most difficult cases, a return to first principles can salvage your work. No manuscript is so chaotic, disorganized or opaque that it cannot be dramatically improved. Solutions, if sought for in an appropriate manner, will be found.

A primary tactic is to go back and refresh your recollections by reviewing the sections of this document appropriate to your specific dilemma, making sure to include the one titled REVIEWING STORY STRUCTURE.

THE 'STEP' OUTLINE

A wonderful tool for rewriters or anyone whose business it is to analyze stories, such as editors or reviewers or story 'dowsers' like myself, is the so-called 'step' outline. This step is a simple procedure in which the writer lists every scene used in the story sequentially.

Whether screenwriter or novelist, it's usually an eye- (and brain-) opening procedure. Scanning your manuscript in order to list whatever action takes place, i.e., writing a sentence for every occasion where something **actually happens** in your story, can have a bracing effect.

It works as follows: you may list not just physical action, such as an entrance, an exit, or one person striking another, etc., but other, equally consequential actions, such as a character determining, say, to lie. Or planning to steal a kiss. Or vowing silently to pack up and leave at the very next insult. Or...? The possibilities are clearly endless.

As the step outline grows, it will soon become apparent whether the story being outlined is dynamic or not.

If, instead of dialogue, conversation is taking place, which, however witty or brilliant, does not result in any movement, the step outline may not be added to. If descriptive sentences, no matter how exquisitely written, do not perform one of Aristotle's three functions—advancing the story, defining character, or creating atmosphere—then no additions can be made to the step outline.

If page after page of the manuscript is scanned and the outline does not grow appreciably, the writer will quickly come to understand that there is more than a little danger, even at this early point, that a reader will be suffering from ennui, if not actually out like a light (the bedside one, that is).

Reading a step outline where the story advances only by fits and starts, if at all, can make it all too painfully clear as to where the problems of the manuscript lie. If you've played fair, it will be obvious by the paucity of sentences on the page(s) which sum up your story.

If still uncertain (read: in denial), grab hold of that mythical teenager (in yourself, if no other is available), read the step outline aloud, and the response will undoubtedly confirm what you have already sensed is the dreaded truth.

The problem areas become self-evident. A half dozen, twenty, even thirty or more pages of your manuscript having been turned without being able to add a sentence to your step outline informs you that even if your story is advancing, it's not breaking any speed limits.

When finished, make a list of those problem areas (adding to those already noted in your prior read-through), then follow the usual routine: pose the problems as questions to your subconscious, sleep on the questions without trying to answer them (your subconscious never sleeps, otherwise there wouldn't be dreams), wake up and get to work. At some point in the morning, answers will be there.

Repeat the process as often as needed.

HOW MANY REWRITES?

It can't be stated often enough: a manuscript is not 'finished' until the author is certain about the thematic statement his/her subconscious is trying to make.

Though some authors have been known to carry rewriting to extreme lengths—hence clauses in publishing contracts whereby after a certain number of galley changes an author must pay for future corrections—there are many more examples of manuscripts reaching the market prematurely. They've been sent off in an unfinished state, metaphorically speaking.

In my own case, I rewrote the manuscript for *Spring Thaw*, my environmental fantasy about seal hunting (called 'magical realism' by some (I thought of it as a ghost story), off and on for almost twelve years. I knew that I had not yet quite got the story 'right'. Something about the material was off.

Eventually, in some despair, literally at wit's end, I changed the way I was telling the story from the traditional past to present tense, and suddenly not only achieved the kind of eerie atmosphere the material demanded, but understood that what had been most wrong all along was not style or atmospherics but the lack of a clear theme.

The subject, violence, was plain enough. But the theme remained murky. I didn't know what I—or more accurately, my subconscious—was trying to say.

Because in changing the storytelling from past tense to present it was necessary to rewrite almost every line, I soon became aware how one scene and then another and another were inherently contradictory. By eliminating those contradictions, I also could see that what my story was trying to say was that whenever we kill we are spiritually diminished.

What I had done was to clear away the underbrush, allowing the thematic statement to stand revealed.

Any fictional work can be evaluated in this manner to determine what it is specifically about. By judging against this elemental standard even our most splendid authors sometimes come up short. Though most of John Cheever's stories are superbly realized, his novel, *Falconer*, about the troubled relationship between two brothers, does not finally 'work' because it is apparent that Cheever had not fully determined what he intended to say. The story's mixed messages are never resolved. What it needed was one more rewrite.

By contrast, reading Pete Dexter's *Paris Trout* (the name of the protagonist) is a harrowing—and transcendent—experience. A stunning novel about a psychopath terrorizing a southern town, there are startlingly diverse and unpredictably brutal and chilling scenes that seem, for a long while, to be pointless. In the final paragraphs, however, the theme rises inexorably from the page as powerfully specific as an illustration from a medieval monk's Illuminated Manuscript: Those Who Ignore Evil Are Condemned To Be Consumed By It.

Ethan Canin, a brilliant young author, did not find

what his story was about, never mind discovering his theme, until the last third of his exquisitely written, but lamentably unsatisfactory novel, *Blue River.* Meandering as the river he writes about, Canin's prose suddenly takes on a purposeful air when he focuses on the relationship of the two brothers. For reasons that can only be guessed at, but most likely because the quality of the writing is so high, neither writer nor editor, unfortunately, thought it necessary to go back and 'fix' the first two-thirds of the novel.

Jane Smiley's *A Thousand Acres*, cannily using the structure of Shakespeare's *King Lear* as a blueprint for her novel of emotional shenanigans on an Iowa farm, comes a cropper when two-thirds of the way through the story incest suddenly rears its ugly head. Too late, because unforeshadowed—though it could have been easily fixed with one more pass through the early prose and the layering in of hints and omens of what was to come. Though the novel won significant awards, it is, by these elementary standards, unsuccessful.

Then why 'fix' something that doesn't seem to be broke? Because once a subject, and then its theme, emerges, an author has what some might term a heaven-sent and others understand to be a subconsciously sent opportunity to compose his/her opus in a manner to remove all dissonances. S/he can fulfill obligations to both art and reader.

It is no longer necessary to rely solely on performance to seduce an audience. By knowing exactly what the meaning of the material is, the author is able to transcend performance and achieve a profundity that is universally understood.

THE FINAL POLISH

Again, we can look to the Greeks for cogent advice.

As referred to before, to achieve the highest esthetic accomplishment, Aristotle felt that every line, aside from its beauty, should serve a useful function. In his discussion of how to write drama, he posited that every line must do one of three things (or, in the best of all possible worlds, all three things simultaneously): (1) define character, (2) create atmosphere, and/or (3) advance the story.

But Aristotle's advice should not be limited solely to playwriting. These strictures should be applied to all fiction writing.

Instead of looking upon them as onerous, the writer should think what an abundance three options for every line is! If none of these specific options fits, the author should cut the line forthwith—yes even if, or particularly even if the line is beautiful.

Every metaphor and image of Jack Casey's *Spartina* has been borrowed from the environment of the novel, a near perfect example of also using that language to reflect the emotional state of his characters. And of course, as referenced earlier, Robert Penn Warren's *All The King's Men* is a brilliant example of how every word serves to create atmosphere, reveal emotion (characterization) and advance the story by using every literary device imaginable.

An author should look upon the rewrites, the cutting and polishing of prose, the way Michelangelo looked upon chiseling stone. What the sculptor saw in the uncut marble were groupings of figures struggling to emerge. By cutting, a writer frees up, or unshackles, ideas; by polishing, a writer can make certain the line performs an Aristotlean function.

It is remarkable, too, how easily a non-functioning line can be 'adjusted' so that it performs—as long as the writer is clear going in as to what the underlying theme is!

By eliminating every line that does not work, in the manner suggested above, a writer may be left with very little, but, paraphrasing Spencer Tracy contemplating a slender but otherwise attractive Katharine Hepburn, "there's not much there, but what there is there is cherce."

IV

THE ART OF STORYTELLING

OPENING LINES

First lines of stories set the tone for everything that is to follow. Of paramount importance, they should be considered accordingly.

"Call me Ishmael," frequently cited from Herman Melville's *Moby Dick*, is great not only because Ishmael is the biblical namesake of the first social outcast, which tells us from what station in life the events being narrated are observed, but it's also technically effective because Melville wastes no time in introducing his narrator.

The reader does not have to know who the original Ishmael was, or even the name's biblical context, to sense the significance of an outcast as the narrator. When creators of any work have thoroughly immersed themselves in the context, their choice of words, conscious or not, will reflect that context subtextually, and readers will intuit its meaning.

Stephen Crane, whose influence can be seen in Hemingway's work, was a master of the opening line.

"None of them knew the color of the sky," from Crane's *The Open Boat*, turns out to be the story of shipwreck survivors, whom we soon learn are too exhausted even to look up from where they're slumped over their oars.

"The Lieutenant's rubber blanket lay on the ground, and upon it he had poured the company's supply of coffee," from *An Episode of War*, sets the tone for an Army company in dire straits.

"It was the fault of a small nickel-plated revolver, a most incompetent weapon, which, wherever one aimed, would fling the bullet as the devil willed, and no man, when about to use it, could tell exactly what was in store for the surrounding country. This treasure had been acquired by Jimmie Trescott after arduous bargaining with another small boy." From *The Carriage Lamps*, these heavily ironic lines, like all of Crane's beginnings, foreshadow events to come.

In each of these openings, Crane not only sets the emotional tone of how the main characters in each story **feel**, but has also established the presence of himself as omniscient author—as does Charles Dickens in the universally known "It was the best of times, it was the worst of times..." from *A Tale of Two Cities*.

In adapting work for the screen, the writer must not only take into consideration the impact of the first words that are spoken, but must also make sure the first images displayed are metaphorically correct.

In adapting my own novel, *The Collaborator*, a post-holocaust thriller set in 1967, it was apparent that the words which open the novel would lose their effectiveness if transferred literally to the screen.

In the novel, the first line begins, "He stood apart from all the others," and goes on to describe a scene in an airport lounge on the eve of a quasi-official Israeli trade delegation's return, the first since the holocaust, to Germany. The line is intended to underscore the isolation of the protagonist, who will soon be accused of having collaborated with the Germans, and cannot defend himself, as he has no memory of his life before 1940.

In the screenplay, which opens with a plane-high

view over the desert approaches to Jerusalem, showing the detritus of the 1967 Arab-Israeli war, it establishes not only the context, but a metaphor for the story's subject, which is about the violence men inflict upon each other. (For more specific details, including an excerpt from both novel and the screenplay, see A SHORT EASY COURSE IN SCREEN WRITING, below.)

PACE AND STYLE

Both pace and style stem from the story being told. It should be evident, though sadly it is so often not, that when a story is meant to race toward its conclusion, paragraphs, sentences and words necessarily become shorter. As a reader's eye is encouraged by the style to move more rapidly along, so too will the reader's pulse.

It should be obvious that complexity of phrase is not conducive to speed.

When writers' goals are to create a dramatically satisfying, and perhaps even explosive ending, it is counter productive to continue to write the same convoluted sentences and densely textured paragraphs that typified their styles at the beginning.

Pace depends upon more than the length and complexity of sentence structure, however.

If a situation is not inherently dramatic, if what has been established does not create a sense of anticipation on the part of the reader, the shortest sentences and the punchiest words will not help much, if at all.

Writers can learn much from the observation of events in everyday life. When engaging in social discourse writers should seize every opportunity to observe audience reaction.

During the telling of a story (any story, anecdote or

joke) be aware as to whether your listeners seem to prefer inhaling another hors d'oeuvre instead of listening intently to your **oeuvre**. Instead of hanging on your every word, do they continually glance over your shoulder, surreptitiously check their watches, edge away?

When invited to a friend's home, does your host begin to tidy up while you're still talking?

Is your Eve more interested in her apple than she is in your efforts to amuse her?

More formally, writers would do well to attend live theatre, where the connection between the drama and audience, instead of merely imagined, can be viscerally felt. Particular attention should be paid to where scenes begin and end. Listen for audience reaction.

Watching a comedy, does sudden laughter drown out the next line, either because spoken too hastily by the actor—or not allowed for by the author? Do you long for a scene to be over with? Or, conversely, do you wish the scene would never end? (Unlike the best novels, which provide the luxury of allowing you to reread splendid paragraphs and scenes over and over, plays, being truly existential, can be savored only at the moment of presentation.) Do you rush back to your seat after intermission?

Perhaps it's no accident that one-act plays are coming into fashion—too many audiences find no compelling reason to return after intermissions.

PAST OR PRESENT: WHAT TENSE TO USE?

Most stories are written in the immediate past tense. Use of this tense brings a significant point, strikingly useful for the author, to the forefront. Events in the story being told have already happened. It is a tale recollected in tranquility, though the remembered emotion may be rendered whole.

Because the tale being spun has, by definition, already occurred, authors cannot (or should not) equivocate, wander or deviate from the events at hand.

Unfortunately, in contemporary fiction, this desirable outcome seems to be honored more in the breach than the observance. Too often, instead of exploring the material before beginning the manuscript, writers attempt to find story and theme while doing the actual writing, thus creating a feeling of uncertainty throughout the manuscript.

Much fiction today is told in the present tense. That obviously suggests that the events of the story are taking place even as the words describing them are being written. This does bring an immediacy that is difficult (though not impossible) to be gotten any other way. In clever hands, the portents, omens and foreboding indigenous to drama can still be utilized.

But the present tense has drawbacks, not least of which is a pretentious air. This occurs when writers adopt the tense because it is literarily trendy, without first considering whether it is appropriate to the story.

In my novel, *Spring Thaw*, the environmental fantasy previously discussed, I adopted the present tense only in a last ditch attempt to create the kind of eerie atmosphere the story demanded. In *Captain Jett*, on the other hand, a historical comedy about race relations on radio during the depression years that I am currently working on, since it is a tale told in retrospect, use of the present tense would prove counterproductive.

Readers are rightfully put off by what is demonstrably illogical, whether above or below the line (of consciousness.) The present tense is, after all, an artificial device.

How can a line like, say, "I saunter heedlessly across the oozing tundra, barely aware of the cry of the randy moose behind me", actually be written while the events are supposed to be taking place?

Poetic license or literary convention aside, writers should, as always, consider what kind of story they are telling, and what benefits, if any, accrue from adopting a tense which is demonstrably artificial.

POINTS-OF-VIEW REVISITED

It is astonishing how often writers, even those well past the early stages of their careers, shrink from the chore of choosing what point-of-view to use in telling their stories. Many adopt the p.o.v. of a single character on the mistaken assumption that it is the easiest, only belatedly to discover, somewhere down the line (when it is far too late), how confining it is.

First person narration, in skilled hands, can be enormously flexible—Robert Penn Warren's brilliant *All the King's Men* is a case in point—but in the uncertain hands of beginning writers it is too frequently limiting.

Writers too often forget that the narrator is not (or should not be) themselves, but a character they have created. Every technique used in creating and defining a third person character must be utilized in the first person as well. A good and simple test of whether this is being done is for the writer to change the p.o.v. from first to third person, from I, to he or she, and observe whether the characterization thus far written is sufficient.

Those who are intimidated by the mere thought of an omniscient voice, thinking it reserved only for the God-like, yet yearn for the flexibility of multiple points-of-view, often try to tell their stories with many but separate narrators, losing the benefit of an overall p.o.v.

But this approach raises as many problems as it solves. The reader, blithely unaware that the first narrator is not the only one (or frequently not even the main one!), is not only startled, but probably put off when a second narrator, without forewarning, is suddenly introduced, contradicting earlier expectations.

How to apprise that reader, after introducing a second narrator, if there is to be yet another and/or still another, without creating the impression that the author is not to be trusted?

Typography can be useful in such cases, such as the device, astonishingly simple, of putting any new narrator's name as a heading atop the chapter being narrated.

Or there can, and perhaps should be, a prologue (or a preface, if the events are being recounted in an expository manner), told omnisciently, that is, narration by the author, in which all those who will be narrating the story itself are gathered (either as children, or adults present at a major event, a wedding, say, or a funeral, or a reading of a will, always an occasion for the releasing of passionate emotions.)

Once again, the important thing is for the author to establish a pattern, making it easy for the reader to follow. Those who claim that they write only for themselves should be asked whether their stories are actually bottom-drawered without being shown to anyone? And those who believe a reader's task ought to be made as difficult as possible, for reasons of literary oneupsmanship, should have long since set this book aside as irrelevant.

The omniscient p.o.v., however much it may seem the most intimidating and complex, offers the most freedom for the writer. Once understood, the o.p.o.v. becomes uncommonly flexible.

The most common problems are easily overcome. Take the trait so many writers have of opening a story inside a protagonist's head. He or she is thinking a certain way about somebody or something. Not a bad ploy in and of itself—but the pattern seemingly established is that the entire story will be narrated from inside the protagonist's head!

But what happens when the author decides it's time to get out of the protagonist's head and into someone else's? Not only are the reader's expectations thwarted, but the author is confronted with awkward and frequently insurmountable obstacles to rendering other points of view (including the author's own.)

A simpler way, as mentioned, is for the author to remember Ernest Hemingway's famous dictum: tell them (readers) what the weather's like. That is, the author describes the environment. Then when the character is then placed in that environment, the reader becomes aware that someone other than the character is narrating the story. That other, of course, is the author.

Next, describe the character's emotional state (that part not already deduced from the environmental description, said description being nothing less than a reflection of the character's emotional outlook, see *All the King's Men* above.)

By these simple acts of description, done from outside the character's head, the author has established an omniscient presence who, either overtly or indirectly, is commenting upon the material.

By establishing omnipotence, the author takes charge. Becoming godlike, s/he reassures the reader that whoever is telling the story knows everything there is to know about what took place when, and what the motivations were. S/he can move into and out of one character or another's head whenever convenient or conducive to dramatic storytelling. An additional bonus to this increased flexibility is that whenever interest in a character or situation lags, the author can merely switch to another.

It is not necessary, though it can be useful, to wait for chapter or scene breaks to go into or out of one or another character's head. Once demonstrably in charge, an author may simply insert (after a character's name) words such as so-and-so **thought, felt, remembered,** etc.

If an author persists in choosing separate p.o.v.'s as a device in telling the story, it should be remembered that with each shift in narrators the story should continue to advance. Only when doing a Rashomon kind of story, in which different characters observe the same events from contrasting views, will readers accept stories which remain static.

FLASHBACKS, FLASHFORWARDS, ETC.

In New York publishing, as in Hollywood film making, both Oz-like kingdoms, editors and producers seem to speak with a single voice. Those who have been down those yellow brick roads far enough, eventually discover, when pulling the curtain aside, that the Wizardly speaker is a fraud, mouthing platitudes in a manner which is designed to obscure the fact that the words are empty of meaning.

So it is with the periodic Hollywood pronouncements that flashbacks are a no-no. (Yes, indeed, baby talk, to be sure, but an accurate reflection of the way Hollywood deals with writers.)

Fiction writers, however, tend to use flashbacks as major events: remembering a murder, say, or a seduction, or a betrayal.

In fact, we all have flashbacks moment to moment in our real lives. In the course of any day we think back to this morning, or yesterday evening, or even an hour ago, in scenes with bosses, clients, lovers, or incidental encounters which have turned out unfavorably.

What triggers these flashbacks is remembered emotions, to wit: shame, embarrassment, passion, and so on. Because we recall events not as dry case histories, but as full of specific emotion, flashbacks should be recollected only as a result of an emotional trigger. Period.

If there is a reason other than a character's emotional state for a flashback, it's probably attributable to the author misperceived notion that exposition is needed.

Remember, only the agendas of the story's characters have priority.

Flashforwards, obviously the reverse of flashbacks, are rare, but can be effective. A classic example is Ambrose Bierce's *Incident at Owl Creek Bridge*, in which a man being hanged visualizes the life he would have led (were he not being hanged, of course). Bruce Joel Rubin's motion picture *Jacob's Ladder* borrowed a similar structure, to brilliant effect.

Science fiction writers, (as in the works of Jack Finney), use their freedom to explore time in all its aspects, frequently including forays into the future.

But it should be kept in mind that if there is not a present time and problem as a story base, futuristic forays become boring.

No matter how spectacular the special effect, if there's no point, what's the point?

COMMON MISTAKES

The distrust of simplicity is the single most common mistake writers make. Whether style, story line, and/or theme, less is frequently more.

Many writers fear their writings will not be taken seriously if they are not intricately structured, multi-themed, or subtle to the point of obscurity. Others believe narrative prose cannot be demonstrably beautiful unless it is elaborately decorated.

But see how often the opposite is true. A statement achieves greater power if made without embellishment. "Beware the Ides of March." "We have nothing to fear but fear itself." "Ask not what your country can do for you; ask what you can do for your country." "So many owe so much to so few."

Or, simply, "I'm going to kill you—not now...when you least expect it."

No need for name-calling, or raised voice; empty threats are those most likely to be swollen with obscenity.

Uncertainty about the story is revealed when an author provides too many "delicious asides" and goes off on tangential issues instead of sticking to the main line.

As for a multiplicity of voices telling an already complicated story it is not so much compelling as confusing, a mob personality instead of an individual's.

More than a single theme leads to incoherence, not profundity.

But how to recognize these problems in your own work, or that of others?

One way, as discussed in an earlier context, is cutting. Take a page of your manuscript at random and eliminate every word which goes beyond a rudimentary function. Read what's left on the page aloud, to yourself, (or to our mythical intelligent teenager), and discover what, if anything, has been eliminated that was necessary to understanding.

If, in trying to explain your work's theme or subject, to the teenager, or, by putting it on paper in a synopsis, you find yourself saying "it's about **this**, and it's also about **that** and **the other thing**, discard **that** and **the other thing**, and see whether your story doesn't take on more power, not less.

YOU'LL NEVER GUESS WHAT HAPPENED AT THE BATTLE OF THERMOPOLAE!

I once sat for almost three hours at a performance of Sam Shepherd's *Lie of the Mind*—the play was well-cast, contained fascinating characters, had strong situations, possessed lots of energy, a lust for revenge seeming to be the overriding theme—and then a character came in at the end and explained how wonderful it was he'd encountered the villain and beat the living crap out of him...and then the curtain fell.

The high point of the play, the so-called obligatory scene, had taken place off stage!

With the plethora of people involved in play productions, I think the audience is entitled to ask where the producers, the dramaturg, the actors and the director were while the play was being put up on the boards? Didn't it seem strange to anyone that the climactic moment of the play was to take place in the wings?

In Australia, most of my energies were spent in encouraging writers to put their conflicts center stage instead of keeping them off where they wouldn't disturb anyone.

Australians, in spite of the loutish image some of

their writers seem to enjoy promoting, are in my experience a diffident lot, having inherited the repressed nature of their English predecessors. Their outback mentality only emerges after too many toppings-up. The successes that were achieved came about when the writers learned to allow their subconscious partners a voice in the proceedings.

EMOTION, AND ITS LACK

The author should not, at least in the first draft, assume that the reader will pick up on whatever emotions the characters may be feeling without first making it clear what those emotions are.

Lack of emotion, either in the characters, or the manner in which the author regards those characters, is high on the list of common mistakes.

A refuge in ambiguity, in the erroneous belief, as earlier discussed, that either (1) readers welcome opportunities to 'fill in the blanks' as a way to participate in the creative process, or (2) readers are enchanted, if not mesmerized, by obscurity, is, at best, disingenuous.

More than likely it's an indication that the author is also uncertain, or too chary of the work required to explore how the characters would react in a specific situation.

We would need to know, for example, how deep the love of a father for his child for us as readers to be affected if, upon hearing news of his child's death, the father expresses no outward grief.

We cannot be expected to deduce at a repressed emotion simply because of how we might feel upon receiving similar news. It is the author's job to create both character and context in such a way that we understand why the grief is being repressed; i.e., family or conditioning by a culture that frowns on emotion; or a refusal by the character to confront reality, who instead withdraws into denial.

At some point (if the story or that character's behavior is to have any point—remember the process is a search for meaning), we would have to see that emotion finally expressed, either subtly, as with silent tears, or more overtly—turned inward, as a suicide, say, or outward, with an act of violence toward another, man, beast or inanimate object.

On the other hand, stoicism, or repressed emotion, on the part of author or character, may be effective, but only when it is made clear to the reader what kind of emotion actually exists!

This came to me in the manner of a revelation while working on a biography, *The Shoe Leather Treatment*, of a patient, Bill Thomas, who escaped after nine years in an institution for the criminally insane. Victoria Pasternak, my editor (at Tarcher/St. Martin's), went through my first draft (actually the second, my first drafts are too 'rough' for submission), and marked every page (sometimes every paragraph on that page) with questions about what emotions the character was feeling.

The result was this (told first person, so nothing would dilute the emotional impact between reader and subject):

"I didn't understand why they had put me here with the babblers and droolers and guys who were just plain out of their minds. I wasn't like them. I was in for an assault I didn't commit. I knew something was wrong with me. I felt disturbed. But I didn't know how to tell anyone what it was that was disturbing me, since I didn't know myself.

"I knew other people thought breaking into mausoleums and opening caskets was really bizarre. I could see really strange looks coming over their faces when they heard what I'd done. But I couldn't see why my trying to get in touch with my Dad was so wrong. He had reached all the way from the other world to punish me by letting my daughter Beth Ann be born retarded. I knew that if I didn't get in touch with him and get him to forgive me even more terrible things were going to happen.

"I got very depressed. I started hiding under the benches. I had been the same in the garage. I'd crawl under cars when customers came so I wouldn't have to face them. Now I still couldn't face up to my problems so I looked for a bench that wasn't occupied by guys trying to jack each other off or by guys kneeling with their arms over their heads, not moving for hours, or by guys walking back and forth on them, waving their arms as if they were balancing a hundred feet in the air. When I found a bench empty I crawled underneath, balled my jacket up for a pillow, and turned my face to the wall."

LOGIC & COMMON SENSE

At the opposite extreme, as writers strive for ways to inject excitement and uniqueness into their work, they sometimes go over the top, and devise scenes, or a series of scenes, that creates a feeling of inauthenticity, due largely to a lack of logic or common sense in story progression or character motivation. This leads to reader confusion and mistrust.

Instead of forcing characters to do or say things that they would never do, writers would be wise first to consider the most obvious thing those characters might do in any given situation in real life. For in real life, we tend to act in predictable, cliché ways.

Far from dwelling upon the banal, this consideration of the predictable, like reexaminations of cliché, which, as we have seen, are perpetuations of basic truths, can frequently result, with an appropriate 'spin', in scenes of great, and authentic tension.

A young student, writing in a recent seminar of a drug addict's homecoming, did not once refer to the addict or her family even thinking, let alone talking, about drugs or addiction. Instead, her scene dealt with genealogical connections that neither impacted on nor were reflected by the troubled past. This resulted in the creation of an artificial atmosphere, with a consequent diminishment of reader involvement.

By discussions of what might be common behavior in similar situations in real life, we seminarians were able, through the answering of some basic questions, to come up with the following:

What is any typical addict's predominant character trait? Answer: lying. What is a common attribute of liars? Thievery.

Anyone who has had any experience with typical addict behavior, unfortunately common in our society, is aware that addicts lie, cheat, and steal, even, or particularly even, from family and loved ones.

Was our seminar student's created family aware of this? Probably, especially if her homecoming comes after a troubled past.

The homecoming of a liar and thief, even if allegedly reformed, automatically creates a tension that can lead to any number of emotionally powerful scenes (repressed or not, as the author chooses.) Genealogical connections—

three generations of women—which are shoehorned expositorially into the text by ignoring the obvious, can instead be brought in logically, and more effectively, by dealing with the disappearance of a family valuable, for example, passed down from generations past.

Possibilities for emotional complications are thereby endless. Has the addict stolen the valuable, and pawned it? Has someone else stolen it, hoping to discredit the addict? Has it been hidden merely to prevent its being given to the addict for fear temptation will prove disastrous for the recovery?

The possibilities for conflict in any family with more than two members are infinite in the most ordinary circumstances; when a family member transgresses they expand exponentially. And by starting with what is commonly true to life the material is imbued with the kind of authenticity that allows the author to take characters into extremes of behavior and situation that seem inevitable.

From the opposite end of the spectrum, of course, a writer can mistakenly assume that because a story is based on real life it is necessarily credible.

Basing stories on real life does not automatically create authenticity. Sometimes the phenomenon of reverse effect is created. And however much writers attempt to deflect criticism of their work by protesting that the events recounted "actually happened!", acceptance by the reader is not so easily won.

An easy way to test for credibility is for writers to reverse the procedures discussed above, and ask themselves how the incident in question might have been handled had they 'made it up' in the first place.

In other words, because a car accident happens in real life does not mean it should happen in a fiction. If the author invents an accident, there should be a reason for it, even if the reason is nothing more than to show the effects of a random event. In this sense, there are no 'accidents' in fiction.

When 'fictionalizing' a real-life event, writers need not, and indeed should not be bound by the reality, but instead make certain that the 'story' meets the standards for character motivation, story logic and the clarity of theme that have already been discussed.

Some will argue that real life, being messy, incoherent and frequently inscrutable, does not easily lend itself to being placed in neat categories. Nevertheless, the author of fictions should want to simulate real—that is, a living, breathing life—not to imitate it; primarily, fiction writing is an attempt to take the meaning of it.

Writers can, and should, have it both ways. By matching fictional events against real life situations, and vice versa, writers, who perhaps try overly hard to impress the reader with an overreaching imagination, can bring unlikely events down to earth by applying corrective doses of common sense.

By reversing the procedure, that is, by applying artistic standards against real life situations, writers employing fictional techniques as they attempt to bring order out of chaos in the search for meaning, can create stunning effects.

The writer, however, through some or all of the techniques discussed above, must more importantly convince the reader on a **subliminal** level.

The manipulation of structure, which in skilled hands can enhance a story's impact (see once again Pinter's *Betrayal*) can have the opposite effect when mishandled. In those works not written in a linear progression (and *Betrayal* is linearly backward instead of forward in time), writers sometimes create a melange of incidents that are neither metaphorical nor thematic. That is, the incidents are not clustered, or grouped, with any kind of logic.

As we have seen, every story must have an interior logic. When a writer creates a fantastical world, that writer must set rules of order under which that world exists. Even if the writer posits that the created world exists under a chaos theory, that theory must be explicated.

In storytelling, logic and common sense go hand in hand. Where they are ignored, disassociation, leading to disaffection on the part of the reader, results.

In a recent seminar, a participant created a prologue of a dreamer awakening from a nightmare, in which a mysterious person is stalking her, intending to kill. But in Chapter One, the dreamer proceeds about her business without seeming to have been affected in any way by the dream. Not once does the awakened dreamer take note of the fact that she has dreamed, reflect upon the dream's meaning, or try to deduce which person amongst all her acquaintances she imagines her enemy might be—in fact, we have not even witnessed the moment when the dreamer wakens from the dream.

Deprived of the dreamer's emotional state, the nightmare in the prologue seems isolated, as if from another story entirely.

Another student wrote about a troubled young couple who discuss whether the wife should return to her parents' home. It is not until a half dozen chapters later, when the decision is made, that we are flashed back to an emotional scene in which, returning after a hurried elopement, the couple confront the wife's parents, who are distraught to discover their favored child is married to someone of whom they disapprove.

Common sense tells us that the appropriate place for the flashback is when the question about whether to return is first raised by the couple. The author's protest that she didn't want to interrupt the dramatic sequence, which extended over several lengthy chapters, was neither emotionally nor sequentially logical, as demonstrated by the reader's confusion.

How we think in real life has more than a minimal bearing on how our fictional characters think. Poetic license will not overcome a reader's disbelief, based on a perception, usually subliminal, that the behavior is anomalous.

Logic, especially the interior logic, is absolutely necessary if the audience is to be convinced. Neophyte sci-fi and fantasy writers believe logic is unneeded—but if a new universe is to be created, then the rules of that universe must be set; or if it's a story with ghosts, then the rules of ghostly behavior, including by whom they're seen, and how, and why, have to be acknowledged.

When writing *Spring Thaw*, though I do not consciously believe in ghosts, I had to set aside my overt disbeliefs, and wrote the novel under the assumption that ghosts, under the conditions set forth in the novel, exist, under the rules of logic in the world that I created.

BREAKING THE RULES

A famous old saying among artists is that in order to break the rules one must first know what the rules are. (This may, in some cultures, refer back to Shiva, Indian God of Creation and Destruction.)

Appropriately, in order to write non-linearly in an effective way, a writer must, at the very least, know what the structure would be if written linearly.

TITLES

For an author, titles are as important in a subliminal sense as for use simply as 'marquee' value in an overt attempt to attract the reader.

Titles also can—and should—provide a clue to a story's hidden theme (see SECRET STORY above), and/or clearly identify its subject.

Titles must ring true, else they not only risk attracting the wrong readers, with a consequent risk of alienating them, but can misdirect an author into failing to get the story 'right' in the first place. If the title does not accurately reflect the material—or vice versa—it is likely that the audience, having been misled, will either cast the book aside, and, having been disappointed, will create a disapproving word-of-mouth.

Titles can be abstract or straightforward, pedestrian or poetic, but must never bewilder author or reader by giving them a sense of inappropriateness.

When an author, using a 'working' title, finds the story beginning to deviate from that title's meaning, it is an important warning that it is time to take stock about what that 'working' title actually means. Either the story's implications must be reconsidered or the title changed.

If the author is reluctant to change either, it is likely symptomatic of a deeper problem—a failure to have explored the title's attractiveness on a subconscious level (using the techniques of SECRET STORY above) before beginning work.

Years ago, a screenwriter friend, Louis Garfinkle, (subsequently co-author of the original script for *The Deer*

Hunter), adapted Stephen Crane's short story, *The Monster*, for a movie. Crane's story is about a black servant who is horribly burned rescuing his white employer's child during a fire, and is closeted away from public view because of the public's reaction to his terribly scarred face.

A creative director for an ad agency at the time, I was asked to talk to the studio executives about their ad campaign, which they wished to be aimed at a horror audience. I argued—in vain—that such a campaign would attract the wrong audience. Crane's 'Monster' title was demonstratively ironic, and the subsequent film reflected that. But the studio persisted, the horror aficionados came, felt they'd been misled, as predicted, and turned off potential audiences by bad mouthing the film as spurious.

In recent years, the art of title writing seems to have fallen on hard times. Contemporary titles are for the most part reduced to two words, not counting the subjunctives **A**, **An**, or **The**, and, when all else fails, authors (and/or their editors) fall back on verbal shorthands, abandoning mythic references.

Where today are the *Appointment in Samarra's, The Lottery, For Whom the Bell Tolls, This Side of Paradise, The Wapshot Chronicles, Tender is the Night, East of Eden, Butterfield 8, The Red and the Black, The Red Badge of Courage, The African Queen?*

V

ADAPTING YOUR WORK FOR STAGE OR SCREEN

SHOULD YOU? WOULD YOU? COULD YOU?

SHOULD YOU? Though horror stories about the movie experience for writers are in abundant supply, most might say the money is worth it.

Others, those valiant and not necessarily misguided few, will make the attempt in an effort to preserve their work's integrity during its transfer to another medium.

Whether for money or integrity's sake be advised that in certain circumstances, enumerated below, both may be achieved—though admittedly, in the preponderance of cases, the integrity part survives only in somewhat diminished form.

As for the money part, agents familiar with the turf usually advise following the bird-in-hand philosophy; i.e., the more you can get up front the better; what's promised at the other end often turns out to be fool's gold.

While on the subject, it might be well to get the negatives out of the way first, on the theory that knowing your opponent gives you an edge in the game. Or, put more delicately, the more understanding you can acquire of the nature of the beast the more opportunities you will have to domesticate it.

LOVED TODAY, PARIAH TOMORROW

Being on hand to preserve your work's integrity

lasts, in most cases, only as long as it takes to finish the contracted-for rewrite—which, in the movie business, ends about eighteen seconds after delivery (the length of time needed to verify that the requisite number of pages have been turned in.)

It's not unusual for the writer to find that no one above the rank of receptionist, not even the assistant to the assistants, is available to speak with you—and certainly no one will ever return your calls.

Once contact has been broken off, it's anybody's guess what's happening to the work. Unfortunately your darkest fears are likely to prove correct. Following the law of averages, your script will be worked on by several additional writers, both credited, and those whose contributions to the script remain, under guild rules, anonymous.

Do not allow yourself to become depressed over this. Count your money, savor the pages of your narrative fiction—your original vision survives; in another form, true, but intact. Be pleased that as a result of your efforts, something of your original vision has at least a fighting chance of shining through.

To avoid this assignment to purgatory, you could, of course, have insisted contractually on being given the right to fix whatever objections there may have been to the first draft by performing the first rewrite—assuming that when your narrative fiction was bought your representatives had either sold your services as screenplay adapter, or at least managed to attach your own adaptation as an inextricable part of the material, whether they wanted it or not.

Difficult as it may be to understand, there are occasions when your screenplay, even if given away without additional charge, is unwanted—it has to do with on-screen credits, which, like everything in the film business, have as much to do with money as with ego. A subsequent writer is easier to sign on when there are no prior drafts—and thus no locked in credits—cluttering up the scene and diminishing potential income.

Keep in mind, however, that in the beginning the original author has the advantage. During the opening negotiations, buyers' mouths are full of butter. They're ardent swains—we loooove your material, it'll make a grrrreat film, we loooooooove you, you are a magnificent writer, not since (fill in the blank here) has a writer of your splendiferous imagination come this way...

Writers, in constant need of reassurance, are easy candidates for such unctuous flattery. Who wouldn't want to believe? But don't fall for it, or for any subsequent dialogue which implies that if you're too intransigent about the deal's terms they may look elsewhere.

No one is ambivalent about material—they love it or loathe it, the intensity either way depending upon the 'package' (a director + actor(s)= multi-$$$) they can envision, and not as a result of any esthetic judgement.

It would also do well to remember that almost no one in Hollywood, other than 'readers', actually read manuscripts. What they read is 'coverage,' i.e., a synopsis plus comments, and sometimes not even that.

The bookjacket of Roderick Thorp's exciting novel, *Nothing Lasts Forever*, which depicted scenes of helicopters attacking a skyscraper, was brought to producer Lawrence Gordon by an assistant who exclaimed, "You've got to read this!" "No, I don't," the producer replied. "Buy it!" The *Die Hard* movies resulted.

By attaching a screenplay to your novel, you make it nearly impossible for subsequent rewriters to 'write you off' the screen. Under current Writers Guild credit arbitration rules (at this writing having survived assault by 'assignment', or self-styled 'greenlight' writers), in order to share credit, at least fifty percent of your screenplay would have to be changed. To write you off the screen credit takes seventy-five percent, which would remove almost all the reasons for your work's having been purchased in the first place. Though not an unknown circumstance, it is thankfully still rare.

But once your screenplay is part of the deal, no one can deny they've had 'access' to your screenplay; contractually, you've made yourself part of the 'loop.' Credit arbiters and/or courts, should it come to that, will not accept protestations that subsequent writers "did not look at the material." If available, it will be assumed everyone 'looked' at it.

By retaining a co-credit, you have also ensured yourself a share of residual monies that accrue from any success your film may enjoy—and you won't have to watch the pathetic spectacle of rewriters accepting Academy Awards for Best Adapted Screenplay not acknowledging the source work their screenplays were based on!

(For a summing up of some principles of negotiation, see ENTERING THE MARKETPLACE, below.)

COULD YOU?

A more difficult question. How to tell if you are capable of writing a film drama?

Setting aside for a moment the matter of content (with very few exceptions, any story, repeat story, can be translated to stage or screen.) Dismiss the canard—we're not talking *a la orange* here—that a work is too 'inner-directed' for a visual medium. Even a portion of James Joyce's *Ulysses* was successfully transposed to the screen.

Could you? Probably—if you don't allow yourself to be intimidated by the technical aspects, or the seeming impenetrability of the marketplace for Hollywood or Broadway and its variant venues.

Writing is writing is writing, as Gertrude Stein might have said. Aside from the obvious differences in format, the constraints of live theatre and film simply call for the use of a different format to achieve the same end: entertaining an audience. Surely the artist in you welcomes the challenge?

The first step in deciding whether your work, or you, have an affinity for the transposition, is to examine your pages from a typographical standpoint.

LOOK AT THE PRINTED PAGE

What do you see? Full pages of prose without a paragraph break? Sinuous sentences, with copious uses of semicolons and commas? Extraordinarily long words, which, upon closer examination, might occasion a trip to the dictionary, if not the encyclopedia, for definition? Little or no dialogue sprinkled throughout the manuscript?

Taken separately or together, probably not the best of signs.

Sentences that run on and on and on without paragraph breaks, chapters so long they might be miniature novellas, and a paucity of dialogue are indications that the writer may be terrified or contemptuous of the spoken word, and have little regard for, or ability to pace. These instances suggest the writer may be of the school that believes more is more.

Obviously, dialogue and pace (foreign films to the contrary notwithstanding) are of paramount importance in translating material to stage or screen. Movie audiences in particular become notoriously restless at the lack of conflict or story advancement.

Novelists who avoid dialogue, who write about what people say in a passive sense, as in a narrative such as:

> 'Lulu, who wasn't feeling all that pleasantly disposed toward her mother, told that concerned lady that she was going out with her loutish cousin Charlie no matter what the consequences might turn out to be',

instead of having Lulu snarl,

> "Save your breath. You can tell me I mustn't sleep with cousin Charlie till hell freezes over and I'll do what I want and damn the consequences!",

movie people probably would be right in assuming that the novelist in the first instance is more interested in his/her own 'voice' than anything the characters might say.

Though the former may fit your work, be of stout heart. All is not yet lost. Remember that William Faulkner's novels sold very few copies during his lifetime, yet he made a handsome living writing screenplays. Those who hired Faulkner were aware that, without exception, his novels possessed a strong narrative—that is, incident driven—drive.

Even today, serious film makers—as contrasted with schlockmeisters (and if you need a definition of that word you may not be ready for Hollywood) are not only willing, but actually prefer giving the storyteller a chance at adapting his or her own work, believing that whatever was exciting about the work somehow has a better chance of being translated to the screen intact by the original writer.

David Puttnam, a British producer of such splendid

films as *The Killing Fields*, and, briefly, head of Columbia Pictures, felt it was important to stay with the original writer—if whatever problems a script had couldn't be solved, Puttnam felt there was little chance adding writers remote from its conception could.

Schlockmesiters, on the other hand, want no part of the original writer. Totally self-aggrandizing, these are people who want to use original material as a springboard into the big casino, hoping to lock into the orbit of a high-flying director or star.

One way to gauge the artistic integrity of would-be purchasers is whether they're willing to give the novelist an opportunity to write a first draft screenplay. Those who refuse out of hand are likely not as interested in the material as the deal, and they'll do whatever it takes to make the deal work. Hence, the legendary Hollywood wisecrack, "Shoot the deal, it's more interesting than the script."

On the assumption then that you have the courage to enter Minataur's Cave, the next step is to examine the work itself more closely.

Take a look at what the words actually say to see if they provide more hints as to whether you're equipped for the journey. If your characters do speak to one another, is it contentious or conversational? Revelatory or expository? Does it conform to Aristotelian precepts, that is, does it define character, create atmosphere, or advance the story?

This kind of work and self-examination is also an essential step for those writers who do not already have purchasers for their fictions, but believe that by adapting their own work they will have a better chance in a lucrative marketplace.

TRY TO BE OBJECTIVE

After you've allowed yourself a few delicious moments to marvel over the lyricism of the narrative, the sheer tear-producing beauty of the words, ask yourself how you're going to translate that marvelous prose to the screen.

Let me put the fact to you plainly: in a script, narrative descriptions aren't made to be appreciated, only to be serviceable. Compression is everything. A few telling words suffices for atmosphere or character. Action is described in the kind of rush you want the audience to feel.

Put another way, it's important to find out how visual your book is. Can you actually picture the scenes in your story? Is the action described in such a way that each incident can be visualized? Do the characters spring to life because of what they say and do?

STARRING ROLES?

Now ask yourself whether you've created starring roles. Does your protagonist drive the action? Or, as is too often the case, is your protagonist someone to whom things happen?

If the latter, that has to be changed—and if you can't, or won't do it, some hired gun of a writer the producers assign will be happy to do it for you.

Whom would you cast as the protagonist? Can the actor you've been fantasying about see her or himself in the part?

Finally, how dramatic is your book? How suspenseful? Have you lit a fuse so the audience holds its breath waiting for the explosion at the end? Is there a moment when the star not only gets to chew the scenery, but to destroy the set as well? Think about how many films you've seen where the star shoves a row of bottles off a bar or pulls down a bookcase or heaves a pail or a person through a window...

What about the structure of your story? Can you divide your story into acts, natural or otherwise, preferably three?

Don't confuse this arbitrary three act structure, by the way, designed solely to enable you to get a handle on your material, with those story consultants who may tell you feature films fall into five acts and TV movies seven—that's for the commercial breaks. For now, suffice it to know that essentially the Greeks had gotten it right.

Remember: Act I states the problem, Act II complicates it, Act III resolves it. What could be simpler—or more effective?

If your story can't be structured in this way, then it may be necessary to change your story so that it can.

When you were first beginning to write your novel, if you didn't experiment with various ways to begin and end it, and if, during the writing process, you hadn't juggled scenes back and forth, trying to find the most effective way to tell your story, now's the time.

VI

A SHORT EASY COURSE IN SCREENWRITING

If, in spite of my urgent advice to write the novel first, you are convinced that the story you have in mind is best—or only—suited for the big screen, then review the various procedures (including SECRET STORY) discussed throughout these ruminations. All that has been said so far about storytelling is applicable to all forms of dramatic fiction.

Once you have these precepts firmly in mind, proceed to your screenplay.

Basically, screenwriting is easy. All a writer has to do is project a movie on the screen in his/her mind, then write down everything that is seen and heard. What could be simpler?

Don't believe it? Consider an underlying work that might go something like this:

> The mountain rose out of the snowy plain, immense and forbidding, a place of impenetrable cliffs and sharp crags and deep abysses. A tiny figure, ill-equipped for climbing, crawled along the sheerest precipice nearest the peak, fumbling for almost non-existent hand and foot holds with frost-bitten, blood-smeared fingers.
>
> Because the sounds of the climber's agonizing struggle caused hardly a ripple in the oceanic silence, the rifle shot, and its echoes, sounded loud

as an artillery barrage.

For a terrifying moment the climber embraced the rock face like a lover unwilling to let go, then, as if accepting the inevitable, released his grip. Tumbling down the mountain, he bounced from crag to boulder to cliffside, eventually disappearing, with a piteous cry, into a bottomless abyss.

The silence returned. The mountain remained impassive.

From behind a distant boulder near the precipice another figure, in full mountain gear, emerged. She (for this hunter was female) chambered another bullet into the rifle.

Look into any collection of screenplays and you'll see that putting the above narration into the proper format for a screenplay would be simple, as follows:

EXT. A MOUNTAIN—DAY

A MALE FIGURE, ill-equipped for climbing, struggles to reach the top. A GUNSHOT, followed by ECHOES. Figure freezes—one beat, two.

FIGURE FALLS, BOUNCING against boulder and crag as he TUMBLES down the mountain, eventually DISAPPEARING into a BOTTOM-LESS ABYSS.

HEAR A DESPAIRING CRY, DIMINISHING
INTO SILENCE.

From behind a boulder ANOTHER FIGURE,
dressed in mountain gear, carrying a big game
hunter's rifle, EMERGES.

As OTHER FIGURE chambers another bullet into
the rifle SEE FIGURE is FEMALE.

And so on. You'll notice there are no CAMERA
ANGLES, no CUT TO's, no indications whether the camera is shooting LONG SHOTS or CLOSE-UPs. The format above is for a feature film, not a television movie
(which makes different demands upon the writer).

BIG SCREEN, LITTLE SCREEN

Don't confuse big screen movies with those made
for the little screen. TV network movies are essentially
plays. They're talking heads rather than talking pictures.
Even cable movies, because of budget constraints, lean more
to words than pictures.

Though the basics of good storytelling remain the
same for both, the details are different. Anyone who's witnessed the results knows why it's said that the devil is in the
details.

In television, it's a writer's medium. Every shot is
described, and directors are expected to follow the script.

In features, the opposite: it's a director's medium.
The patently ridiculous *auteur* theory aside (any dictionary
defines the word as creator, originator, etc.)—the main reason for this is that the director has the responsibility for
transferring the script onto film. **Falling Upward**, the phe-

nomena of a director going from one failure to another, is because the director has demonstrated that he has been able to actually get a finished film up there on the screen.

A collaborative art? Of course.

A fitting, if simplistic, analogy would be to compare movie making to what happens in advertising agencies: copywriters come up with the concept, hand it over to art and TV directors to make it visible. But where, in advertising, and in television, power has been retained by the conceptualizers; in features it has flowed to the director.

Thus even if shots are described, directors can, and do, ignore them. Writers are expected only to provide the master scenes and dialogue. A screenplay is considered a blueprint, agents package it, directors and stars (sometimes the same person) take over the reins.

In the hands of a director like Robert Altman, or a star whose clout is larger than his/her brain, even dialogue is used only as a general guideline, ludicrous in professionals whose success was achieved using other people's words, not their own.

If you're lucky, you'll fall into the hands of the rare director who, when confronted by a star who doesn't like—for whatever reasons—the lines given, calls in the writer for a conference. After all parties agree to a scene's intent, the writer rewrites the lines to fit.

SILENT SCREEN TECHNIQUE STILL WORKS BEST

Though the technology has exploded, particularly in terms of shoulder-braced (so-called 'hand-held') cameras and on-screen pyrotechnics, the addition of the spoken word hasn't changed the writer's basic task all that much. It's more likely to be pictorial images, rather than the dialogue, that influences the audience most.

Even in those dim distant days which, thanks to cable, are no longer beyond recall, audiences could tell by the pictures what was going on, and what the appropriate dialogue, if any, would be.

When the distressed maiden recoils from the unwelcome advances of the mustachio-twirling villain, we don't really need the insertion of an ornately decorated placard to inform us that the gist of what she's saying is, "Unhand me, you cad, your advances disgust me!"

Notice how these characters, though stereotypical, behave in very characteristic ways toward each other. In contemporary terms, they're 'acting out' in a way that's revelatory of their deepest feelings.

It's always been a necessity of script writing to describe a character not in terms of how that character looks, but what their personalities are. Thus:

INT. FIGHTER'S GYM—DAY

Smoky, grimy walls, FIGHTERS in protective helmets sparring in a ring. JOE MCKEE, a self-centered, so far unmarked young pugilist, suddenly catches his SPARRING PARTNER, a beat-up aging fighter, with a left hook and a right cross.

As surprised opponent DROPS, Joe leans over him at the ring ropes to address HOWIE CASTELLI, a down-in-the-mouth fight manager whose careworn face reflects all the fighters he's watched dive into the tank...

JOE
Plenty more where that

came from, Mister Castelli—
if I had a manager like you
there's nobody could stop me!

It's important to know what each character's dominant characteristic is. Call a character charming, sweet, sour, delightful, mean-spirited, or whatever. By clearly delineating the character, you not only give the 'reader' important information as to how the character may react in sure-to-come story situations, but give the film makers important clues as to how a role ought to be cast.

You also provide a 'handle' to the actor. In addition to counting the number of scenes they're in, actors want a quick fix, unambiguous, on who their characters are. It's all right to say that a character is confused, as long as it doesn't confuse the actor.

As stated before, it is unfortunate that in Hollywood almost no one who has the power to 'greenlight' a movie knows how to read. Those who are assigned to the task as readers have little or no experience in actually mounting a play or film. Hence William Goldman's famous admonition that the writer should write two scripts, one for reading, one for 'shooting.'

Those assigned to read (and analyze) material tend to skim the descriptions, and concentrate on the dialogue. Though I'm not recommending the writing of two different versions, the descriptions had better be brief, and the dialogue needs not only to delineate character and create subtext and advance the story, but create drama as well.

"It was a dark and stormy night", Bulwar-Lytton's notoriously bad line appropriated by Charles Schulz' insightful cartoon strip *Snoopy*, is not inappropriate for a screenplay. It's all the director needs to set the scene.

Dialogue, however, carries a heavier burden. The best dialogue is intense and compressed as poetry. Profanity, though useful as a device to individualize character and as an indicator of the build-up of tension, is too often these days sprinkled indiscriminately throughout a script, like rank weed, apparently in the hopes that no one will misidentify the script as designed for anything save the big screen or cable.

A bigger problem is misusing dialogue to deliver information. There is no place for expository writing anywhere in dramatic fiction. A screenwriter must be as ruthless about this as a director is with film. The best film directors, like the best writers, discard any scene which does not advance the story. When in doubt, follow Elmore Leonard's lead, and leave out everything that readers skip.

Television movies of the week are the worst examples of expository writing, no doubt because they are almost always the products of committees stacked with 'development executives'. Afternoon 'soaps', on the other hand, for all their faults, thrive on conflict, and are often better examples of lively dialogue than prime time commercial television.

Commercial television rarely buys a completed script. Scripts are 'developed' from ideas. Thus we watch patchwork stories that barely hold together, written by writers who either haven't learned their craft, or are forced to write scenes that conform to 'notes' imposed by development executives.

All too frequently, we watch characters not only telling each other what they already know, but describing their own psychological makeups to each other. These clumsy attempts to provide the audience with information demonstrate a lack of craft.

The term 'dumbing down', though made in reference to the audience, says more about those who make such statements than those they are talking about.

Audiences, even if marginally literate, are hardly dumb. If sentient, audiences can, and will, intuit what's going on. It doesn't take a genius to understand what a raised voice, eyebrow, or fist indicates.

Though context is important, we don't need a recitation of *curriculum vitae* to understand that a character is well educated. An armload of books indicates a certain level of studiousness, a stethoscope in a pocket indicates a doctor, an expensive business suit a level of success, a tattoo on an older person reveals lower social status (on a younger person rebelliousness), and so on.

To repeat an earlier admonition: the only specifics an audience, stage or page, needs to know should be provided only when the characters in the drama need, or demand to know it.

DIALOGUE FROM PAGE TO SCREEN OR STAGE

Dialogue that works on the page rarely works when transferred to the screen in its original form.

The legendary exception, of course, was Dashiell Hammett's *The Maltese Falcon*. Allen Rivkin, a screenwriter who shared offices and a secretary in a studio writer's building with John Huston, realizing the novel was the equivalent of a screenplay, took a red pencil and marked the book's pages up accordingly. It fell into Huston's hands. The resulting film is the novel visualized.

Most novels don't translate so readily. Because visual images cannot replace all the nuances of narrative text, the dialogue, instead of merely functioning to highlight a prose narrative, or as more modern versions of those inserted placards, carries some additional burdens.

STRENGTHENING THE VISUAL MUSCLE: SOME EXERCISES

Writers who want to strengthen their ability to produce visual, as contrasted with literary images might try seeing how many pages of a screenplay they can write without having anyone speak. Learning to make do without dialogue is enormously helpful in showing how a character's behavior may be used both as revelatory of personality and in advancing the story.

NO NARRATION, PLEASE

As, or if, you find difficulty advancing the story with only visual images, do not fall back on 'narration.' Neither should you use narration in a misguided attempt to retain the lyric quality of your prose. Thinking that audiences will be mesmerized by the sheer beauty of your language is self-delusion.

If you feel your story must be narrated because your protagonist does not participate in the proceedings so much as observe them, be advised that such a passive protagonist works even less well in film writing than it does in novels.

If there's one rule—beyond whatever works—that pertains to all fictive writing, it's that the protagonist must push the action. This rule becomes absolute in film writing, because what actor wants, or is able to, play a passive character? And if the protagonist is pushing the action, how much room can be left for palaver?

Very few films are conceived with a narrator in mind. If a movie has a narrator, you can bet the family inheritance that when the 'final cut' was presented to the studio, the consensus among the executives was that audiences wouldn't get it. A sure way—they think—for audiences to get it, is to have a disembodied voice explain it to them.

But narrations, with few exceptions, are not only admissions of failure, they're esthetically wrong, thus counterproductive. Because narrations almost always wind up explaining what is actually being shown on screen—that is, explanations of the obvious, they're boring. By intruding on the audience's collective imagination, they lock out a major contribution to an audience's enjoyment, their own participation.

The great exception, of course, is Billy Wilder's and Charles Brackett's classic *Sunset Boulevard*.

The film opens at night on a legendary Hollywood mansion, and come in on a dead body—a writer, I'm sorry to report—floating in the swimming pool. We hear the dead writer's voice, and he is going to tell us how he wound up dead. There is hardly a better story hook, or a better use of flashback, anywhere.

Most people who insist on narrations, almost always after the fact, don't realize that not only must they make it an integral part of the material, but that it must be logical as well.

Case in point is the narrator of *The Year of Living Dangerously*. The character who narrates—played by the diminutive actress Linda Hunt—dies halfway through the film. Who is telling the rest of the story?

Another example of a narration which misses the mark is the Martin Scorcese-directed *Age of Innocence*, from the novel by Edith Wharton. It is doubtful that those in the audience know—or care—who the person is doing the narration. Because the voice is female (in actuality Joanne

Woodward), we eventually deduce that it's the voice of Edith Wharton. But the author is not a character in this tale.

While an author can and should be a stylistic presence in novels told omnipotently, such a device comes a cropper in films.

If, instead, the narrator of *Age of Innocence* were, say, the eldest son, who has an emotional stake in the outcome of the story about his parents' thwarted love—if they hadn't married he wouldn't exist—it would give resonance to the proceedings, and add a layer of suspense presently lacking. As a character in the story, we would assume the narrating son will eventually have reason to confront his parents. With the story having a destination, the audience will be roused from its torpor. As it stands now, with no clear protagonist (who is it about?), and no resolution (what is the movie's theme?), the audience walks out dissatisfied.

HOW TO START?

You can be reasonably certain that the way your story starts on the page is not the best way to start your story on the screen.

Before I offer an example from my own work, a brief history: my screenplay adapted from my first published novel, *The Collaborator*, a post-holocaust thriller, resulted from the fact that a generous and gifted director, Ralph Nelson (*Lilies of the Field*), gave me the opportunity to hone my craft by allowing me to learn while doing, and kept me on the project until I got it right. (The treatment was 200 pages, almost as long as the novel, and the first draft screenplay was 180 pages! Several dozen rewrites later (most recently this year, for a European-American co-production), I got it down to its present 118.)

The way the novel opens is:

"He stood alone. The others all had wives, children, brothers, sisters, cousins, friends, subordinates from their departments, and of course, inevitably, the newspaper reporters, swarming about them."

The setting is the main airport in Israel. A quasi-secret trade delegation is on its way to Germany, Jews first return since the holocaust. A Nazi-hunting Israeli investigator, Kohn, arrives to arrest the man who conceived the mission, Gottliebsohn (who "stands alone"), on suspicion of having been a collaborator in Germany in 1939.

The accused can neither confirm nor deny the charge—everything before 1945, when he arrived in the land which became Israel, is a blank. There's an argument. The mission is allowed to continue—accompanied by Kohn, who will conduct the physical investigation, while Dr. Glass, an American Jewish psychiatrist (presumed to be 'neutral'), will investigate his mind.

Not much visual stuff there to open a movie with. Here is the screenplay:

FADE IN:

EXT. THE DESERT (Plane-high view)—DAY

Hot. Desolate. A trail, littered by the debris of war—gutted tanks, half-tracks, abandoned shoes, a corpse uncovered by the vagaries of the shifting sands.

COME INTO a terraced valley, PASS OVER a kibbutz.

EXT. JERUSALEM—DAY

INTO the City through the Arab quarter. Title identifies JERUSALEM—1968. SEE TOURISTS, young ISRAELIS in shirt sleeves, side-curled Hasidic JEWS in long black coats and black hats, burnoosed ARAB VENDORS, uniformed ISRAELI POLICE.

ON APARTMENT BUILDING

OUT of which COMES ERNST GOTTLIEB-SOHN, a strong, self-contained but melancholy man in his mid-forties, dressed too formally for this desert city. But not only his starched collar and worn attaché case set him apart—it's his wary manner as well.

OTHER ANGLES—GOTTLIEBSOHN

marching along the narrow street. URCHINS scramble out of his way—he does not notice. Neither does he notice:

KOHN

on the opposite corner, a neat dapper man with a face like a fist. Kohn looks thoughtfully after Gottliebsohn, then slips across the street and INSIDE the apartment building.

INT. APARTMENT BUILDING—DAY

Kohn climbing the narrow stair, pausing before door with name-plate (E. GOTTLIEBSOHN.) Kohn makes sure he's alone, slips plastic card between door and lock; goes IN.

EXT. INSTITUTIONAL PLAYING FIELD—DAY

BOYS playing soccer. Gottliebsohn ENTERS, watches.

A boy spots him, then ANOTHER and ANOTHER—boys wave, kick the ball TOWARD HIM (CAMERA.) With some fast and fancy footwork, Gottliebsohn eludes boys and kicks the ball into opposite goal.

GOTTLIEBSOHN acknowledges A CHEER that goes up. Then once again dignified and proper he DEPARTS.

INT. GOTTLIEBSOHN'S APARTMENT—DAY

KOHN opening cabinets in sparsely furnished rooms, searching drawers, finding all almost bare. A Groz-like PRINT (an anguished MALE) is only decoration on one wall;

A PLAQUE on another wall states that E. Gottliebsohn distinguished himself in the fight to establish a Jewish state. Next to an easy chair is a well-thumbed ELEMENTARY HEBREW GRAMMAR.

ON BEDSIDE TABLE
next to spartan bed is water pitcher, glass and pill
bottle.

ENTERING FRAME, KOHN examines, then
pockets pills.

EXT. ARAB QUARTER (ESTABLISHING)—
DAY

CAMERA FINDS GOTTLIEBSOHN in
CROWD. He slows outside a house. An ARAB
BOY SHOUTS (in Arabic) and leaps to open door.

AT UPSTAIRS WINDOW a painted Arab
WHORE APPEARS, recognizes Gottliebsohn,
motions him to come up.

GOTTLIEBSOHN points to his watch, shakes his
head, walks hurriedly OFF.

INT. GOTTLIEBSOHN APT.

KOHN ENTERS, lifts toilet lid, pees while picking
up another book, a child-simple HISTORY OF
THE JEWS. Finishing, Kohn zips up, goes to wash
his hands—REACTS as he looks at

MEDICINE CABINET has blank space where
mirror should be.

KOHN PALMS space.

EXT. WAILING WALL—DAY
A VARIETY of WORSHIPPERS praying as Gottliebsohn ENTERS.

GOTTLIEBSOHN WATCHES for a time, then, as if pulled against his will, he joins swaying line, stands rigid, then, bowing head, clutching case to chest, he begins, awkwardly, to imitate the others.

Several FLAGGED GOVERNMENT VEHICLES ENTER square, escorted by MOTORCYCLE SOLDIERS. A HASIDIC JEW observes, SHOUTS, picks up a rock. A POLICEMAN is instantly there, an ARGUMENT ensues.

MORE HASIDIM APPEAR; MORE POLICE ARRIVE.

FROM LEAD GOV'T LIMO, AUERBACH, a middle-aged, sardonic diplomat, steps OUT, MOTIONS impatiently for Gottliebsohn. GOTTLEIBSOHN starts toward limo, stops, turns.

HIS POV—POLICE & HASIDIM CLASH. Suddenly get an almost subliminal

FLASHBACK TO:

EXT. COLOGNE—DAY (THE PAST)

A BRIEF FLASH OF GERMAN THUGS and JEWS CLASHING.

BACK TO PRESENT as Soldiers shove G. thru rioters to limo.

INT. GOV'T. LIMOUSINE—DAY

Auerbach and HORTSKY, a white-haired patri-arch) pull G. INSIDE as DRIVER forces limo through CROWD. Angry RIOTERS peer inside, fists pounding on glass windows.

HORTSKY
God save us from religious Jews.

Notice there are five pages before the first line of dialogue is spoken. That sets up the metaphor for the story: Jews at war with Arabs—Jews at war with themselves. By the end of the film we will understand, on a level deeper than feeling, that the protagonist, Gottliebsohn, is a man who has been at war with himself.

OTHER EXAMPLES OF HOW—AND HOW NOT —TO BEGIN A SCREENPLAY

There are probably as many options for opening a screen story as there are in narrative fiction. The writer should remember that the same storytelling rules apply.

Before the titles, a kind of prologue can be done, as in Agatha Christie's *Murder on the Orient Express*. As a kind of game, in workshops, I ask those participants who have seen the movie to tell us how it opens. With almost no exceptions, what most remember is the echoing train sta-tion, and the introduction of the Belgian detective, Hercule Poirot (played by Albert Finney).

The way the film actually opens is to show the kidnapping of a baby, and newspaper clippings about it, all in sepia tones to indicate the past. What is being shown subliminally is the motivation for the murder. Then there are the titles, and the audience is soon so beguiled with the introduction of the various characters (all suspects) in the present that they soon forget how the film actually opened. But at the film's denouement the resolution is twice as strong because the full impact of what motivated the murderers had been absorbed on a subliminal level earlier.

Another brilliant prologue is the way the film version of William Peter Blatty's *The Exorcist* opens. At the archeological dig, earlier discussed, the diggers suddenly break into a crack of the earth, and the hounds of hell are released. Now we're aware that evil is abroad in the land. When we're introduced to our protagonists, we know that they are about to be subjected to great travail.

Or we can see what happens behind the credits as both background and action in consecutive sequence, as was done in *Bonnie and Clyde*, written by David Newman and Robert Benton, which opens with a shot of Bonnie in her upstairs bedroom, vain and bored to distraction; a horn honks, she looks out, and there's Clyde, in his Ford coupe, waiting below. Grabbing her purse, Bonnie's off with Clyde. We don't need a narration to know they're headed for trouble—all established in a very few minutes.

A similar, if less intense opening is Patrick Conroy's *Conrack*, which opens with the protagonist waking; the camera pans Conrack's room, we see his personal belongings (clues as to his character) and watch him feed his parrot, giving us clues as to his personality. By the time he goes outside and gets into his skiff (he's on an island) and rows over to the mainland we're hooked, fully aware that this is going to be the story of an unusual character in an unusual setting, reconfirmed once he enters the school where he's a teacher and we see how the black children react to him. Again, all this is beautifully compressed within a very few minutes.

(*The Pumpkin Eater*, adapted by Harold Pinter from a novel by Penelope Mortimer, introduces a new character solely by use of visual imagery: the camera pans an untidy room, lingers over a piano and a penciled-in composition above its keyboard, arrives at the rumpled bed, wherein resides the female protagonist and her newest lover, who we've already guessed is a composer.)

Another well-conceived consecutive sequence is writer Waldo Salt's screenplay for *Midnight Cowboy*, from the novel by James Leo Herlihy. The cowboy leaves town in a helluva hurry (we don't find out why—a gang rape in which the cowboy was unable to help his girl—until much later, in flashback.) This could have been done, as in *Murder on the Orient Express*, as prologue, without losing any suspense. He catches a bus, and we have a travelogue from Middle America into greater New York, where he encounters Ratso Rizzo.

These two characters, by the way, are extremely self-centered; by the end of the movie, each of them would be willing to give up his life for the other. Both have been changed by their relationship to each other. In its profoundest sense, *Midnight Cowboy* is a love story.

An example, referred to earlier, of a prologue that doesn't work is *W.C. Fields and Me*. The way the movie makers filmed it, we see, before the credits, a trunk stickered with labels of venues from all over the world. A little dog come out and pees on the trunk.

That's a powerful metaphor, but of the wrong kind—what the filmmakers are actually telling us is that W.C. Fields is a man who deserves to be pissed on. When later we see Fields abusing his mistress Carlotta, we haven't witnessed any of his redeeming features, so we hate Fields, and, by extension, because the filmmakers gave us permission, we hate the film as well.

In real life, Fields had run away from home to an orphanage. This suggested to me how the film might have opened: a kid being beat up, before the credits, accompanied by the sound of laughter on the soundtrack, followed immediately by a scene on a vaudeville stage, showing comics hitting each other with water balloons. Next, we could see Fields as a kid being thrown down a flight of stairs, accompanied by a roar of laughter, cutting then to a scene of Keystone Kops beating each other up with rubber billy clubs.

By the third scene of physical abuse accompanied on the soundtrack by laughter, followed immediately by a shot of a laughing audience, we'd know everything we'd need to know about how the character of Fields was formed. Once aware of that, we'd understand why he abused Carlotta. We wouldn't like it, but we would understand it. We would have created a reservoir of understanding full to brimming. We wouldn't hate Fields, would suffer instead for both abused and abuser. It's a form of sympathy.

As for that ubiquitous dog, instead of showing contempt, we'd make him affectionate instead, trying to lavish love on a wary Fields, who is, after all, on record as stating that any man who hated children and animals couldn't be all bad.

Don't, by the way, try to sell 'understanding' to Hollywood as a substitute for 'sympathy'. Sentiment is always more saleable.

BEST SCREEN STORIES ARE COMPLICATED, NOT COMPLEX

Screenwriting's demands aren't all that much different from other forms of storytelling. In all forms the writer ought to establish the protagonist, the milieu, and the tone of the piece as swiftly as possible.

However complicated motion pictures may be, the best ones are never overly complex. The reason so many thrillers fail on the big screen is because they are so convoluted the audience has difficulty following the action line. Movie viewers, unlike book readers, have no chance to pore over the material to discern meanings. Because film moves so fast, it becomes all the more important for the thematic matter to be so focused that the subtext can be intuited easily by the audience.

As for the story line: it was not too long ago that studios advised writers that every quarter of an hour an audience should be reminded of what's happened to date, then told about what will be happening, before going on with what's happening now.

Sounds too simple. It doesn't have to be made overt, it can be as subtle as the writer wishes, or is able to, make it (as long as it's consistent with the no expository writing rule.) Certainly if more writers reminded themselves as frequently about their own story lines, we wouldn't be so often confused about what is happening on screen.

SUMMING UP ADAPTATIONS

Refresh yourself as often as needed about the elements that go into effective storytelling.

Next, approach your fiction with the view that nothing about the structure is sacred.

Taking a leaf from the screenwriter's work book, list every scene on a three-by-five card, beginning to end. This is called a step outline. A cork board—or a blackboard with eraser handy—can be effective in helping the writer visualize the entire span of the potential screen story.

Once the work is laid out before you, eliminate every scene which does not advance the story. That's right, discard every non-functional scene. If you want the luxury of changing your mind later, you can save the card by putting it in a 'maybe' stack. Chances are, however, you will discover later that there is no necessity, hence no place, for it.

Experiment next by juggling key scenes, putting them at different places in the structure, always making certain, of course, that you retain the basic three acts, a complication to rocket you off into Act II, and a similar push to resolution entering Act III. Be alert to the varying resonances that result when scenes are moved; always assume that placing a key moment earlier in the story changes how the story will subsequently evolve.

Remember that background material is the baggage your characters are carrying as they enter your story; all else is prologue. Though the writer should always assume that the audience is ignorant of the milieu in which the story takes place, all we should ever find out about it should be conveyed only by the characters during the course of the drama.

COMPARING PROSE VS. SCREENPLAY FICTION

In prose narratives, it's almost impossible to end a scene at midpoint. Generally, every scene has a mini-structure similar to the overall structure of any drama. There's a beginning, middle and end. Characters must enter and leave. And usually scenes must be concluded before the writer can move on. The trick is to end a scene in such a way that the reader wants to read on, a difficult, though not insurmountable, task.

In screenwriting, scenes are rarely written out to such conclusive ends. Scenes frequently open with characters already in mid-action or mid-dialogue, and can, and probably should be left in similar fashion.

But these moments, brief or lengthy, must be telling: a clandestine meeting, an ominous telephone call, a theft, an eavesdropping or a surreptitious witness.

In a novel, such moments cannot be so simply rendered. Attention must be paid to transition lines, scene and character description, and so on. The screenwriter's job is by definition seemingly easier. Furthermore, leaving a scene mid-beat not only adds to the suspense, but increases the speed of succeeding events, no small accomplishment.

But in screenplays, as in novels, the juxtaposition of scenes is equally important. How scenes feed into one another provides resonance, as long as the writer always keeps it in mind that every scene has a part in advancing the story.

Match cutting—ending one scene and beginning another with shots which are so similar they enhance the power of each—does not seem much in style today. Either our writers have lost the art, or the directors have. A shame, because such cuts can be very effective.

A famous (among film buffs) moment in Robert Bolt's magnificent *Lawrence of Arabia* is where a close-up of a wooden match, struck by a thumbnail, flares into flame, which is transmogrified by a match cut into a glorious sunrise.

Most would probably wrongly assume it to be a

directorial moment; director David Lean has publicly credited it to Bolt's script.

Those writers who are clear about the relationship between theme and content will find it easier to come up with such magical moments.

SUGGESTED FORMAT FOR SCREENPLAYS

Though specifics may vary somewhat from studio to studio, there is a general format which pretty much suits all.

When you first introduce a character, the name should be in CAPITAL LETTERS. Afterward, use only upper and lower case. In some formats, PHYSICAL ACTION & SOUNDS are also CAPITALIZED, though overuse of this makes a crazy quilt of the text.

Unlike manuscripts for novels, script dialogue and descriptions are single spaced; double space only after scene headings and shifts, shots and cuts.

Master scenes are different locations, identified as INT. for interior or EXT. for exterior, and whether it is day or night, as in EXT. LOURDES CATHEDRAL—DAY, followed by a double space, and then a description of what is happening at the location.

CUT TOs or DISSOLVEs are no longer necessary, though they sometimes can help clarify a time shift.

SHOTS, if used, should be CAPITALIZED, followed, after a double space, by its description. If you wish to indicate SHOTS without ANGLE ONs or ON CHARACTER's NAME, simply start a paragraph with the CHARACTER'S NAME CAPITALIZED, followed by a lower case description of what's happening, such as JACK DASHES toward the car, finds it empty, DASHES OFF.

It should go without saying that the script should be made as entertaining and easy to read as possible. If it seems absolutely necessary to write lengthy scene and action descriptions, at least paragraph them—a good rule of thumb is to double space every three lines.

Finally, neatness counts. A well-typed, typo-free, grammatically correct script in any medium is a sign of professionalism. As in publishing, no dot matrix printers, please—those dots dizzy the eye.

SHOULD YOU? (REVISITED)

Good arguments can, and have been made on both sides of the question as to whether a novelist ought to take the plunge into adapting his own fictions. Hemingway never did, nor did Tom Wolfe. On the other hand, Fitzgerald and Faulkner did.

When asked how he felt about Hollywood having ruined his novels, James M. Cain, in a classic response, replied that his novels weren't ruined, there they were, up on the shelf, just as he had written them.

Stand-off? Maybe not.

Some artistic benefits may accrue: re-thinking a narrative fiction as a screenplay will probably make future narrative work more visual. Cross pollination—borrowing from the devices and techniques of each form for use in the other—can enhance both.

My novel, *The Boss's Wife*, had its genesis as an original screenplay, written for a producer whose failure to meet certain deadlines caused the rights to revert to me. I decided to do it as a novel before sending it to market again.

In the process of going from screenplay to novel, more or less in a reversal of the procedures described above, I discovered, somewhat to my surprise, that the story had gotten deeper, richer, better.

While there are instances of original screenplays

achieving a kind of profundity, the vast majority never achieve the heft and depth of a novel. The very nature of the medium does not allow for the exploration of character and event usually demanded by a novel. What is demonstrably superficial in an original screenplay becomes the tip of a subtextual iceberg in one that is adapted, producing resonances where all was echo-less before.

Today, it seems many writers, particularly in Los Angeles, think first about screenplays.

Leaving aside the fact that what seems a glittering marketplace probably has less chance of producing payoffs than a lottery, I am convinced that anyone who has a terrific idea for a movie should write the novel first. This doesn't mean foregoing the medium. It simply improves a writer's chances of creating a story that will work for both.

DO NOT GIVE YOUR MONEY AWAY

If the esthetic arguments are not enough, consider the other rewards that await.

Why should some overpaid hack get more bucks for writing the film adaptation than novelists get for book rights? Where were they when the page was blank?

Assignment writers boast that without their work, films would not get 'greenlighted.' But without your original story, they would have nothing to work on.

A chicken or egg situation?

Hardly in this case. First the laying of the egg, then the scramble.

THEY'LL TRY TO DISCOURAGE YOU

Chances are, if you've never written for stage or screen, they'll try and discourage you from making the attempt. There will be talk about the special demands of the form that only experience can provide, the special relationship an assignment writer with multitudinous credits has with director, star or studio. If you persist, they may even threaten to withdraw their offers to purchase your material.

Of course even if they agree, there are no guarantees that platoons of writers might not eventually be hired to rewrite your precious script. But once a first draft is in place, at least the core of the story has a better than even chance of remaining.

NO ONE WANTS ANYTHING JUST A LITTLE BIT

In an industry where no has a hundredfold more power than yes, if someone actually has indicated a willingness to pony up money for your work, there's a major deal probably lurking somewhere in the background.

Of course you can't be sure. And here is where you have to be tough. It's difficult. You want so much to see your novel transferred to the screen, pocketing the bucks that entails, even if in the translation only you will recognize anything from the original material, it's difficult not to take the money and run.

If you decide to take a stand, however, you must assume your insistence on doing first draft screenplay may indeed be a deal breaker. Console yourself that at least you will have gone down with all flags flying.

If the idea of coming up empty-handed is too much for you, there is an alternative approach.

If all else fails, and they simply won't pay you to do the first draft, then throw it in for the price of the story buy.

MAKE FIRST DRAFT FREE PART OF DEAL

That's right, make the first draft screenplay part of the action—no additional payment on their part.

THEY MAY NOT BE DELIGHTED

Don't be surprised if they do not seem to be delighted by your generous offer. More times than not, they do not want your screenplay even as a gift.

Why? Because once you give them a first draft screenplay based on your work, it's almost impossible for your name to be eliminated from the on screen credits— since the characters are of your invention, and the story was developed by you. Since the most the producer's lover, nephew, or son-in-law can do then is share a credit, you're going to get residuals. Got that? Residuals. And a splendid health plan for a year. And membership in the Writers Guild film society. And the companionship, and envy, of those writers who…the list goes on and on.

That's right. There are bucks involved. And there is at least one good reason the original writer should share in the potential riches.

To sum up: Would you? There are more pros than cons. Could you? Examine your written work. Should you? If you think you can, the view from here is, absolutely. Go for it!

VII

ENTERING THE MARKETPLACE

AGENTS

The first two questions most often asked at workshops and seminars are (1) Do I need an agent in order to submit material? And, even after hearing about small presses and those few large publishers who accept unagented material, want to know (2) How do I get an agent?

Agents serve as unofficial screeners, or, in a manner of speaking, editors-at-large. It's an agent's job to keep up with the demands of the marketplace, and to have enough judgement to know whether your material can fill those demands.

For the most part, studios and production companies also want only agented material, though in some instances will accept unagented material as long as it is accompanied by a statement that the writer will forego any legal claim against the company.

Robert Bookman, a principal motion picture agent at Creative Artists Agency in Beverly Hills, once said that "If you're good enough to have me as an agent, you don't need me as an agent."

Don Congdon, my agent, whose agency represents both major and minor literary figures whose common denominator is an effective and coherent writing style, says "Literary agents represent a writer's literary business; therefore a writer needs enough business to warrant representation." Congdon does not solicit clients, though he and his associates will look at manuscripts that come recommended.

On both coasts, lists of reputable agents are easily obtained. *Literary Marketplace* lists literary agents, and in New York there is an official association of literary agents. The Writers Guild of America, East and West, have lists of agents that are accredited with them.

The ability to write a query letter is an essential tool for the writer who wishes to acquire the services of an agent. Like the jacket for a book or the poster for a movie, a good query letter should intrigue and titillate; it must, in very few words, give the essence of the material you wish to have read, presented in a manner that will in a very real sense 'showcase' both your talents and your book/movie/play.

If you cannot come up with this kind of query letter; if you cannot write the bookjacket or poster, then it might be a good idea to go back over the precepts recounted earlier in this text—there is a distinct possibility that the material is not yet in shape to be presented.

For those, finally, who simply cannot switch hats from creative artist to huckster (though I have tried to show how we are all, in a sense, continually 'selling' our stories to the audience, grabbing them, metaphorically, by the lapels), then you may wish, as a last resort, to consult an attorney.

Russell Baker once suggested that since the U.S. had so many attorneys, and Japan, conversely, had so many Toyotas, that to balance the trade gap we should trade attorneys for Toyotas.

Almost everyone has access to an attorney. Have the attorney submit your material to publisher or production company. It will give a kind of official imprimatur to the submission; you will seem, at least for those moments before the reading, professional.

PROTECTING YOUR WORK

Our copyright laws do not protect ideas, only their development. (Which explains, perhaps, why so many good ideas are not done so much as 'done in' on television.)

But not to worry: as our fingerprints and our DNA's indicate, no two of us are exactly alike, as a result of which, none of us develop stories in a similar way.

This is easily proved by tossing out an idea to any group of writers and witnessing the incredible variety of stories that come back in return. Or, more simply, play the gossip game: at any gathering, whisper a secret in your neighbor's ear, and try to recognize that secret in what you hear back from the last person in the room. (Probably tabloids are written in a similar fashion.)

It is unfortunately true, however, that there are thieves amongst us. In Hollywood, where writers swarm like locusts preying upon the literature of the land, ideas are swallowed whole, and a measure of caution is suggested.

The easiest, most effective way to protect ideas is not to tell anyone about them until those ideas have been realized in a completely developed work.

Remaining silent has a side benefit. Writers should be aware that every time they talk about their idea before it is written will find their enthusiasm for doing the actual work is diminished accordingly.

As writers, we write to be read, to be appreciated, to be stroked. Every time we tell someone our terrific idea, and receive any kind of favorable response in return, our need to put it down flags somewhat. Enough stroking, and we may lose the desire to write that particular idea at all.

Therefore when friends ask, "What are you working on?", the answer should be given in only the most general terms—"A novel, it's about the human condition." And, if pressed, suggest that what they are asking is similar to querying about the condition of your bowels, or the number of sexual encounters you might have in a day.

An even greater risk to bruiting your ideas about is getting an unfavorable reaction. "Is the marketplace open to that?" doesn't do much for the sense of confidence essential to the writer.

The wisest course is to write the completed story before telling the idea to anyone. Repeat, anyone (including spouses or friends.) When finished, simply send a copy of the manuscript to yourself by registered mail—and do not open the envelope. The postmark, and the unbroken seal, verify the date it was completed.

Or, if you wish an official documentation, you may apply for a registered copyright at the U.S. Copyright office. The Writers Guild also has a registration service.

What you're doing is establishing the date of completion. Under current U.S. copyright law, your manuscript is automatically copyrighted as it's being written. The trick, of course, is to prove it.

Because it's difficult, if not impossible, to protect an idea, most disputes revolve around the issue of access to the material where the idea has been developed.

Writers should keep records about every meeting in which their stories are discussed. A good way to enhance the record is to follow up every meeting by sending a note to the participants recapping the meeting, making sure to identify the ideas and material(s) discussed, along with any new ones you may have tossed into the mix.

Putting the recipients on notice that there is a written record that they have had access to the material may dissuade them from 'borrowing' your idea and imbedding it into a 'new' and 'completely different' development.

It may preclude any need for lawyers; if there comes a time when you need them, your lawyers will bless you for your foresight.

VIII

MISCELLANY

WHAT ABOUT WRITING GROUPS?

While writing is by its nature a solitary occupation, writers can be helped by joining writing groups, particularly in the early stages of their careers if—and this is an important if —certain rules are followed.

(1) Do not give stories to the group's participants to be read at home. This makes the participants editors/collaborators/competitors instead of audiences seeking entertainment.

(2) Choose a strong moderator, who will not allow cross-talk or questions. Positive responses should be encouraged. Instead of an interrogation, those commenting should limit themselves to expressions of curiosity, which might include the hope that certain unrevealed information will eventually emerge. The writer/victim should remain silent, limited to a spoken, if not heartfelt, thank you at the end of a discussion.

(3) The moderator should allow only a minimum of "hitchhiking" on other comments. Criticism builds on criticism. Like piranhas, the longer critics are encouraged to feed, the more frenzied they become.

(4) Comments should always start with what is liked about the work. This is not designed to mislead the author about shortcomings, or to soften coming blows. Since not a lot can be done about an author's weaknesses, it's more helpful to concentrate on that author's strengths. The more

authors become aware of, and utilize their strengths, the more their weaknesses will tend to disappear.

Nos are more powerful, and less helpful, than yeses. For some reason, those who are negative are infrequently asked to support their views, but when someone's enthusiastic, we always insist on knowing why. Unlike our justice system, the burden of proof shifts to the defense.

Critics are never in short supply. The late, great operatic tenor, Lauritz Melchior (whose son, Ib, many also know as a fine writer of spy thrillers), once sang in a performance of *Die Valkyrie* in which the brunhilde was less than good. Opera lovers will recall this opera has a scene with a horse. In this instance, whoever was supposed to have purged the horse had neglected to do so. The horse entered, and purged itself.

Silence. Mr. Melchior stepped forward to confront the thunderstruck audience, shrugged, and said, "Everybody's a critic."

(5) Group participants should try to listen as readers, not as writers. It's an important distinction. Those with different notions of how a particular idea ought to be developed should keep it to themselves. Criticism of the writer's style should be kept to a minimum as well. Eventually, the writers of the most purplish prose, through fatigue if nothing else, will begin to limit this excess—or may wind up as hugely successful writers of romance or horror.

Participants should give the writer their reaction to the story itself, paying particular attention to hints which may have begun to reveal the story's theme; afterwards, if what's been read is part of a longer work, impressions of where the story seems to be going can be included.

Writers should always consider, when listening to critiques, that any comment, even if it seems irrelevant, may actually be signalling symptoms of deeper problems. Writers should keep in mind that when agents or publishers, in rejecting material, extend writers the courtesy of saying why they are declining, instead of going into a defensive mode, writers should at the very least look for ways to improve their manuscripts.

A sign of professionalism is to be open to good ideas, wherever from or however they come.

(6) Never, ever attack a writer's overall conception, particularly if being read chapters from a longer work. Gently does it. Writers' egos are fragile at the best of times, and though stubbornness may be an unattractive trait, its cousin, persistence, is not. Participants can prove most helpful to the writer by searching out those instances when the writing is most appealing. Observe the golden rule—treat members of your group as you wish to be treated.

THE MOST IMPORTANT RULES OF ALL.

Remember that some of the most important rules for writers are to (2) read everything, (3) write a lot, (4) re-write for as long as it takes to make sure you have the correct *who* (the protagonist) and have identified the *what* (the theme.)

Topping the list, however is the first rule (1) Whatever works, use it.

A prescient and eventually successful writer once observed that with persistence and postage enough, anyone can get published.

An old Hollywood expression suggests that if you wait by the table long enough, someday you'll get fed. A friend of mine prefers the remark attributed to Abraham Lincoln: "If all things come to him who waits, it is only the leftovers from him who hustles."

Talent is what we're born with. What we do with it is up to us.

IX

REPRISING A FEW FUNDAMENTALS

1. Writing about what you know best means writing about what you feel. All else is research. Love, hate, sorrow, fear, disappointment, hurt, ecstasy and rage all reside within the author; facts can be found in encyclopedias. Emotions connect writers with readers, conscious with subconscious.

2. Write about your novel before writing your novel. Writers who make it up as they write along create the same uncertainty in readers as is felt in themselves. Remember: most stories are told as if after the fact. Foreshadowing is impossible unless the writer knows what's going to happen; it's during the process of outlining that the writer takes on an air of *authority*.

3. Be wary of exposition. Most inexperienced writers and not a few professionals "warm-up" by "sliding into" their stories, apparently feeling the reader must be supplied with a sort of mini-history to "set the stage" (this is Prologue), or given the background of the characters (this is Resume.) Of course the writer must know all this, but for use as "subtext," not filler.

4. Remember: first person "I" narrators are characters created by authors. Though primarily witnesses, they should also serve as catalysts for the final denouement. Narrators without emotion are usually without character as well. By showing emotion, narrators function as conduits for releas-

ing the emotions of the reader.

5. Every character should have an 'attitude'. This includes the author. Readers respond viscerally to obsessed characters whose wants drive the action. Obsessed characters need not behave violently; they may, in fact, be gentle souls. But even the meek may want something badly enough to drive them to extraordinary behavior. Passive characters too often merely reflect the author.

6. Remember Aristotle's proposition: every line of a drama should do at least one of three things: advance the story; develop (deepen) character; establish mood. Perhaps only one-tenth of published fiction attains this ideal, but this does not negate the principle. Test each line to make sure it is pulling its load. If a line, a paragraph or a page, no matter how exquisitely written, does not perform one of these functions, get rid of it.

7. We know we've been told a story when a character changes. In relationship stories, characters change each other. Secondary characters should not only affect the main characters, but the action as well.

8. Look for conflict whenever your characters talk to each other. Dialogue is conflict between people made tangible, and is only superficially connected to how we talk in real life. Conversation is not dialogue. Extraneous small talk, however colorful, is dull in real life, duller on the page. (See Fundamental #1.)

9. Once an author understands the point of a scene, it needn't be stated for the reader to get it! Show, don't tell,

which means no exposition. Deliver information only when one character seeks out information from another. Once information has been delivered never deliver it again unless it changes through distortion—by a lie, say.

10. Once a gun is shown it must be fired. Never betray a reader's trust. Red herrings are a sign of author weakness. Play fair. In fiction as in life, arousing expectations which remain unfulfilled can lead to unfortunate consequences (such as frustrated readers.) Remember: in a mystery every suspect should have sufficient motivation to have committed the murder.

11. Clichés state universal truths about the human condition. Thinking in terms of cliche helps to decipher themes below the surface in your material. Remember: reinvigorating a cliche may be as simple a task as rephrasing it, such as Robert Penn Warren does in his *All the King's Men* 'He turned white as a starched sheet'. Do reimagine tried and true devices: narrators, for example, needn't always be alive—think of the writer in *Sunset Boulevard*.

12. Readers want an excuse to root for your protagonist. Self-pity is a turn-off. Characters need not be wholly admirable, that way lies sentimentality. But we should understand them enough to want them to succeed. Look for ways your protagonists can ingratiate themselves with other characters as well as your readers—sometimes it's as simple as having the good cop offer a suspect coffee, or a kleenex.

13. Withholding information frustrates readers. The most effective suspense is when the reader knows, but the protag-

onist doesn't. The pulse quickens to see the heavy behind the door with bludgeon at the ready; or to witness the stalker of the night duty nurse waiting in the bushes.

14. Opening words create powerful images. A character stepping in excrement may be vivid, but look for more positive images to plant in the reader's mind that will reflect more favorably on your material.

15. Finally, never assume a manuscript cannot always be made better. But once the *who* and the *what* are made clear, the rest is polish.

Words, Wise and Otherwise, can be found from the following:

Leslie Abramson
Robert Altman
Aristotle
Fred Astaire
Lauren Bacall
Russell Baker
Robert Benton
Robert Bolt
Robert Bookman
Ambrose Bierce
William Peter Blatty
Charles Brackett
Ray Bradbury
Gil Brealey
Hugh (Timmy) Brooke
Bulwar-Lytton
Ethan Canin
James M. Cain
Jack Casey
Raymond Chandler
John Cheever
Agatha Christie
Don Congdon
Barnaby Conrad
Patrick Conroy
Stephen Crane
Pete Dexter
Charles Dickens
Fyodor Dostoevsky
William Faulkner
Jack Finney
Henry Fonda
E.M. Forester
Sigmund Freud
Louis Garfinkle
William Goldman
Lawrence Gordon
John Graves
David Gulpilil
Dashiell Hammett

Gerald Heard
Ernest Hemingway
James Leo Herlihy
Linda Hunt
John Huston
James Joyce
David Lean
Elmore Leonard
Ib Melchior
Lauritz Melchior
Herman Melville
H.L. Mencken
Arthur Miller
Penelope Mortimer
Moses
Ralph Nelson
David Newman
John O'Hara
Harold Pinter
David Puttnam
Theodore Reik
Allen Rivkin
Bruce Joel Rubin
Waldo Salt
Martin Scorcese
William Shakespeare
Shiva
Sam Shepherd
Charles Schulz
Jane Smiley
Bill Thomas
Roderick Thorp
Robert Penn Warren
Edith Wharton
Billy Wilder
Wizard of Oz
Robert Weverka
Calder Willingham
Joanne Woodward

ABOUT THE AUTHOR

A successful novelist, screenwriter and playwright, S.L. Stebel has won wide renown as a story 'dowser', working as a consultant on novels, plays and feature film scripts for writers, directors, publishers and producers, and is a popular teacher and lecturer at major writers' conferences and universities.

Adjunct professor and writer-in-residence in the top-rated Masters of Professional Writing program at the University of Southern California, Stebel is also a charter workshop leader and lecturer at the world-famed Santa Barbara Writers Conference, and has conducted weekend seminars at various universities, including a master class in Screenwriting at the American Film Institute.

Stebel has himself published six novels for major publishers (notably the environmental ghost story *Spring Thaw* and the post-holocaust thriller *The Collaborator*, now being packaged for a film), as well as a biography of an escaped mental patient, *The Shoe Leather Treatment*, and an exploration of America, *The Vanishing Americans* (serialized in *West* magazine as *Main Street*.)

His one-man show for Henry Fonda, *Fathers Against Sons*, toured nationally to critical acclaim. His play, *Dial 1-4 Sex Talk* was given a notorious production at the famed Actors Studio Workshop, and his dramatic adaptation of Ray Bradbury stories was given its world premiere at the historic Ivar theatre in Hollywood as *Next in Line*.

In Australia, his contributions to the so-called Australian film revolution have been termed significant. Films he worked on (*Picnic at Hanging Rock* and *Storm Boy*) won Best Picture in successive years at the Australian equivalent of the Academy Awards. His original film, *Dreams of Marianne,* was shown at the Cannes Film Festival.

He has published short fiction internationally, and for some years he was a columnist covering the Avant-Garde for the *Los Angeles Times Sunday Book Review*. Subsequently he was appointed its Crime & Suspense Critic, writing the column *Thrillseeking*, followed by the column *Eye Spy* at the *Herald-Examiner Sunday Book Review*.

A former International Secretary for P.E.N. center U.S.A. West, Stebel was chairman of its Fiction Awards for 1995. He is a member of the Author's Guild, the Writers Guild of America, West, and is listed in *Who's Who in Entertainment*.